KENZIE'S RULES FOR LIFE

KENZIE'S RULES for LIFE

Mackenzie Ziegler

G

GALLERY BOOKS

New York   London   Toronto   Sydney   New Delhi

G

Gallery Books
An Imprint of Simon & Schuster, Inc.
1230 Avenue of the Americas
New York, NY 10020

First Gallery Books trade paperback edition February 2019

GALLERY BOOKS and colophon are registered trademarks of Simon & Schuster, Inc.

For information about special discounts for bulk purchases, please contact Simon & Schuster Special Sales at 1-866-506-1949 or business@simonandschuster.com.

The Simon & Schuster Speakers Bureau can bring authors to your live event. For more information or to book an event, contact the Simon & Schuster Speakers Bureau at 1-866-248-3049 or visit our website at www.simonspeakers.com.

Interior design by Bryden Spevak

Manufactured in the United States of America

10 9 8 7 6 5 4 3

The Library of Congress has cataloged the hardcover edition as follows:

Names: Ziegler, Mackenzie, 2004- author.
Title: Kenzie's rules for life / Mackenzie Ziegler.
Description: First Gallery Books hardcover edition. | New York : Gallery
  Books, 2018.
Identifiers: LCCN 2018000839 (print) | LCCN 2018019077 (ebook) | ISBN
  9781501183591 (ebook) | ISBN 9781501183577 (hardcover : alk. paper)
Subjects: LCSH: Ziegler, Mackenzie, 2004—Juvenile literature. |
  Actors—United States—Juvenile literature. | Singers—United
  States—Juvenile literature. | Conduct of life—Juvenile literature.
Classification: LCC PN2287.Z55 (ebook) | LCC PN2287.Z55 A3 2018 (print) | DDC
  791.45092 [B] —dc23
LC record available at https://lccn.loc.gov/2018000839

ISBN 978-1-5011-8357-7
ISBN 978-1-5011-8358-4 (pbk)
ISBN 978-1-5011-8359-1 (ebook)

CONTENTS

- - - - - - - - - - - - - - -

CONTENTS

FOREWORD

I'm pretty much in awe of my little sister. Over the past year or so, she's grown into this incredibly confident, incredibly dynamic, determined young woman who lets nothing and nobody stand in her way. And I'll be honest: The change took me by surprise. I remember baby Mackenzie at our dance studio, totally insecure and crying all the time because she had to be in the back of the routine. I remember her throwing a temper tantrum if I wouldn't play American Girl dolls with her. I remember her hiding behind my mom's legs and clinging tightly to my hand wherever we went. But now, whatever idea she gets in her head, she makes it happen. She doesn't take no for an answer. Case in point: She said she wanted to write a book, and now here you are, reading it. She's kind of a force!

I think the turning point was when she finally figured out who she is and who she wants to be. She found music, she branched out, she discovered "her thing." She found her voice—literally! I'm so proud of her. Of course, I'd be proud of her if she wasn't a huge pop star with an album that I *actually* like to listen to. What I'm most proud of is that in thirteen-plus years, she's never stopped being Kenzie: funny, giggly, goofy, annoying, but also incredibly kind, compassionate, and eager to help others. She has the biggest heart I have ever seen— even bigger than her mouth (and that's saying a lot!). She's willing to put herself out there, which is not an easy thing to do, especially when you're a teen or tween and people are so judgy. I know she went through a lot of hate, people calling her names and trying to knock her down. But she didn't let them. She held her head up, she did her own thing, and now she's even stronger.

Which is why IMHO she's the perfect person to be giv- ing kids our age advice—she's so encouraging, positive, and honest. Sometimes too honest! She'll tell me stuff I don't necessarily want to hear, like, "Hey, you got something stuck in your teeth," or, "You've got a zit on your forehead." But I know she's only trying to help. If I have a problem, I come to her—which maybe sounds weird, because I'm the older one. But she's really good at putting things into perspective and giving them a positive spin. She believes in bringing out the best in people. You can't be around Kenzie and not laugh or smile; she just coaxes it out of you. She is someone who believes that there is light and good to be found in every place and everyone.

I love her so, so much—always have. My mom has a picture of us when she was first born and I'm holding her. She has this full head of hair and I'm squeezing her so tight, her face is as red as a tomato. I just couldn't help it! I was in love! We went through a fighting stage a few years ago, but I have to say, now we're not just sisters, we're best friends. I can tell Mackenzie anything and vice versa, and we're always there for each other. The dynamic of our relationship has changed: I used to boss her around, and now she tells me what to do. But somehow, it doesn't bug me that much. I'm pretty impressed with how she speaks her mind and voices her opinions. When we were younger, I always complained when she would try and tag along with me and my friends. But now I love spending time with her and we're closer than we've ever been— which should make our mom happy, since she was getting a little tired of refereeing.

If you're lucky in your life, you find someone who always

tells you how great you are. My sister has always been that person for me, and I'm proud to be that person for her. So here goes: Kenz, you're amazing! Keep doing what you do, and I don't need to tell you to reach for the stars. You're already swinging from them!

♥

INTRODUCTION

So, I've always been a "go with the flow" kind of girl— when life hands you lemons, you make lemon slime (see recipe page xvii). My mom will tell you I have a "sunny, upbeat personality," and my sister Maddie will agree and insist that nothing ever bugs me. But that's not true—stuff does bug me. Stuff drives me crazy. (Um, Maddie drives me crazy sometimes, especially when she steals my makeup.) But I've always believed that life is what you make of it. You can sit around and mope and complain and feel sorry for yourself, or you can find a way to make things work and have a really great time doing it.

I don't know if you can have a *philosophy* for life at thirteen years old—it's kind of young, don't you think? But I do know that I have certain rules that I live by. For example:

» *Friends are the people who really know you and like you—even when your feet smell.*

» *Haters gonna hate. They have nothing better to do with their time. I do!*

» *If you see it, you can be it: There's no such thing as dreaming too big. My dreams are XXL.*

» *If I'm taller than my mom, I should be allowed to ride in the front seat of the car. Just sayin'.*

A lot of people ask me questions through social media or when they bump into me shopping at the Grove in L.A.—about everything from how to handle embarrassing situations and tips on beauty and style, to boy problems and how to convince your parents to let you stay up late on a weekend (still working on that one!). So I thought I should probably organize my answers and put them all down in one place. A book sounded like a really great idea—a lot of work, but a really great idea! I mean, I would have loved to have had some of these answers handy when I was younger and dealing with all the tween drama. People don't know how tough it is to be a kid these days unless they're a kid themselves. But I get it. I get all the pressure, not just in front of your face at school or at the dance studio, but on social media, too. Growing up and trying to find your way in this world can be tough—I'm still figuring it out myself.

And I'm really flattered when someone comes up to me and wants my advice. I'm glad you guys trust me, because I always try to be honest. Sometimes I might say something silly or put my foot in my mouth (I can actually do that, you know—I'm pretty flexible!), but when someone asks me what I think, I tell them. I remember sitting for interviews with Maddie when we were on *Dance Moms* and she would roll her eyes when I gave my real opinion on something ("Kenzie, you can't say that!"). Well, I just did! I never hold back. I'm never going to be someone I'm not, or act a certain way to fit someone else's idea of who I should be. That's just a formula for being unhappy and unsuccessful, don't you think? It's like being a fake or a phony, or putting on a mask. And I don't mean one of those soothing sheet masks you get at Sephora—I mean one that hides who you truly are. You want to be the best person you can be? Then be *yourself*! Sounds like a good rule to me!

Another thing you should probably know: I don't like to sleep late, which I know is so weird for a teenager. You will rarely find me lying around all day on my couch just chilling. Binge-watching Netflix is great, but it's a rainy-day option only. I always like to be doing *something*, whether it's working, singing, writing, making YouTube videos, rehearsing, dancing, or hanging with friends. Seriously, I *have* to be busy. So I promise you, you will not be bored reading this book—it's filled with so many ideas about what you can do with your day, everything from activities and quizzes to recipes and crafts. I am obsessed with watching craft how-tos on YouTube—I want to try them all. I will literally drag my mom out to Michaels to pick up tons of glue and glitter and crafting supplies so I can make something I saw on a video. She's like, "Kenzie, *really*? This will make such a mess!" and I'm like, "Well, yeah—that's the idea!"

Never let a potential mess stand in your way—another one of my rules. Whether it's a literal mess (like the time I decided to tie-dye my sneakers and wound up tie-dying myself instead) or something that doesn't involve staining the rug, you should do it. What have you got to lose? So you try something you've never done before and it's an epic fail. So what? If I make a fool of myself, I laugh about it. And I don't give up easily. I try it again, and I work harder till I figure it out. Persistence is a great rule for life: You can never go wrong with never giving up.

So you can see how these rules of mine come about. It's a lot of trial and error and doing what makes me feel good, not just about a situation, but about who I am as a person. I hope you read them, try them out if they sound fun and helpful, and then eventually make your own rule book for life, because that's really the goal of growing up. You get to decide what and who you want to be and how you want to go about it.

For now, since I'm only a teenager, I guess I have to listen to *most* of what my mom and stepdad tell me to do (although the rule about making your bed every morning doesn't seem like a keeper). To be honest, my friends and family have always been really supportive and cool about letting me be me. My mom will tell you she's my biggest fan, and I know it, because I couldn't have done any of the things I've done so far without her cheering me on. She was the first person who noticed me singing around the house all the time and suggested I take voice lessons. Now, I'm recording and writing my own music and playing to huge concert audiences all over the world! Who knew? But it goes to show that you need people who are willing to stand behind you and believe in you.

As you read this book, think of me as that person for you. I know you can do whatever you set your mind to. I also know that sometimes things feel confusing and overwhelming and super frustrating, and you'd probably rather just pull the covers over your head and not come out for a week. That's when you take a deep breath and go make that lemon slime. Did I mention you can eat it, too?

☺ Mackenzie

KENZIE'S CRAFT CORNER

"WHEN LIFE HANDS YOU LEMONS" EDIBLE SLIME

have always loved doing artsy projects—when we were younger, Maddie and I had an entire craft room in our house, filled with everything you can think of: paints, markers, construction paper, felt, sequins, glitter, stickers, glue sticks. We never bought a single greeting card—we used to make them from scratch. And my mom kept every DIY birthday and Christmas gift we made her, no matter what it was—and some were pretty bad, like frames and boxes that we glued together out of pom-poms and pipe cleaners, lol. If I couldn't think of something creative, I would make her a coupon—GOOD FOR ONE FOOT RUB! GOOD FOR ONE BREAKFAST IN BED! GOOD FOR ONE MASSAGE!—and cover it with stickers or glitter. My mom would always say it was sweet, but then she would put it in her drawer and forget about it. Somewhere, she has a pile of coupons she can cash in for an awful lot of pampering. Uh-oh . . .

Crafts are clearly my thing. I love the idea of creating something from bits and pieces of something else—magic without the magic wand! Slime is by far my fave DIY obsession, and I am always making different kinds and colors with my friends. I even did it blindfolded once with Maddie. Yeah, don't ask. . . .

WHAT YOU'LL NEED:

* 15–20 yellow lemon-flavored Starburst candies
* ¼ c. powdered sugar
* 1 lemon, cut in half and scooped out clean

1. If you're working with hot stuff, it's always a good idea to enlist a grown-up to help. Place the Starbursts in a heat-safe bowl; then place the bowl on top of a pot of water and set it to boil (if your mom has a double boiler, it's even easier).

2. Once the candies are melted and you can stir the slime easily, allow it to cool for a few minutes so you can touch it and shape it.

3. Place the powdered sugar on a nonstick mat and pour the slime in the middle of the powder.

4. Knead the slime; the more sugar you incorporate, the thicker it will be (and the sweeter it will taste!).

5. Shape into a ball that fits in half of the lemon. You can put the other half of the lemon on top to keep it clean and store it for snack time! This slime is easy to pull, twist, and play with, but also tastes yummy. Genius!

KENZIE'S
RULES
FOR
LIFE

RULE 1
CONFIDENCE IS KEY

"YOU GOT THIS!"

If I had to pick my number one accessory it wouldn't be a cute baseball cap, a cool mini backpack, or even my most comfy pair of Vans sneakers. It would be confidence; it's the one thing you can "wear" every single day, no matter the occasion or place, and it looks good on everyone. I wasn't always so sure of myself. When I started dancing, I was the youngest one on the team, and I always felt like my sister and her friends were so much better than I was—they had been doing it longer and knew the drill, and I was "the baby."

To be totally honest, I didn't even really *like* dance at first, and I didn't feel like I was good enough—at least, not compared to everyone else. They were all so polished and perfect; I felt like a hot mess! I was also really nervous about people watching me on TV—would they laugh at me? Would I look really stupid up there? I knew the cameras would be following us around and catching everything I did and said. It certainly didn't help that for my very first solo, they dressed me in a mouse costume and the tail kept getting stuck when I tried to do my tricks. I was embarrassed and really insecure. Maddie helped me a lot with that. She told me not to worry about what people think, just do you. So that's what I did; I let the real Kenzie come through and suddenly all the nerves and doubts melted away. Which isn't to say they *never* pop up from time to time today—whenever I try something brand-new, I get nervous and I can feel my confidence dipping. But it's okay; if I was super sure of everything, my head would get so big, it wouldn't fit through the door! I think of confidence as a muscle you have to build and flex like you would if you were training in dance class. The more you work at being confident, the more easily it comes.

BELIEVE IN YOURSELF

I have had so many people knock me, insult me, criticize me, tell me I'm not good enough—from people in my own studio, to haters online, to kids I thought were my friends. I guess that makes me kind of an expert on this subject: You can't let anyone crush your confidence. I've also noticed that the more confident you get, the more people who are insecure will try and chip away at your self-esteem—making you feel small makes them feel bigger. Block these people out of your life and just do what you love—you can choose not to listen! I used to think I needed to be a pleaser and make everyone happy, but that's just not necessary—and it's also pretty exhausting. When I did something only because I was trying to impress someone or make them like me more, I realized it didn't feel very good. I wasn't being true to myself. So yeah, maybe they were happier about it, but I wasn't!

It took me almost the entire time I was on *Dance Moms* to get to a place where I was comfortable and confident enough to say, "I know what I want and this isn't it." I was over it. I felt like the constant competition life was getting to be too much. It wasn't fun for me anymore; I was ready to move on and do something else, and I knew my heart wasn't 100 percent in it. That can happen sometimes—it's part of growing up and discovering who you are as a person. Sometimes the things that you once loved and thought were so much a part of you just lose their fun factor. Hey, I used to be obsessed with playing with my dolls, and now I'm pretty sure they're all in a box somewhere in the closet collecting dust. Who would have thought that I'd get tired of something that meant so much to me? For me, leaving the show and the whole dance-team life was a similar feeling: One day, the old things that I always did seemed just that—old—and new things appealed a lot more. Here's the thing: You know "you" better than anyone else. You know what makes you happy or, as my stepdad, Greg, will say, "whatever floats your boat." I guess it was kind of a shocker to my family and definitely my teammates when I said I was done with spending hours a day focusing on dance. It had been my life for so, so long! At first, my sister was like, "Kenzie, you can't quit competing! You're too good now and you're improving every day." But then she realized I was changing and growing, and she supported my decision. She saw it wasn't just me getting bored or tired and lazy ('cause sometimes I get a little cranky and fed up when I am!). It was me knowing I was capable of doing so much more in my life and feeling ambitious and a little "itchy" to branch out. She had been there before, so she got it: I was ready to move on.

CAST A CONFIDENCE SPELL

Okay, maybe I've read a few too many of those Whatever After books or I've gone to Disneyland too many times (is such a thing possible?), but I think believing in yourself is a little magical. You have to have faith that you can—and will—make your dreams come true, because as soon as you do, everyone around you starts buying into it. Why? Because as soon as you start working really hard toward achieving something important to you—in my case, a career as a pop singer, author, actor, clothing designer, and so many other awesome things—people see that you're serious, focused, and determined. You may not succeed at first, but you project a champion's attitude, and eventually that will get you where you want to be. If you can convince yourself that something is possible, it's that much easier to convince everyone else. I remember when I released my very first single a few years ago, I was pretty nervous. I didn't want to put my music out there and have people hate on me for it. I actually tried to picture what the mean comments might be, writing them in my head: "Stick to dancing! You stink!" or "Kenzie can't sing." Then I realized how ridiculous that was: I was sabotaging myself before my album even hit! I told myself that my fans would love it because I was doing it for them as much as I was doing it for myself. I convinced myself that even if the album didn't sell a single copy, I would have tried something new and that I'd be proud of myself for having gone for it. And then something really crazy happened: The single flew up the pop charts and wound up number one on iTunes. I couldn't believe it! I was like, "Wait! Is that my name? Is that really *me*?" Like I said—magic! I know that everything I do won't always be a huge success ('cause that's kind of how life works), but I feel like you always have this superpower in your back pocket anytime you want to use it: your confidence.

• •

5 WAYS TO SUPERCHARGE YOUR SELF-CONFIDENCE

If I forget to charge my phone at night, it dies on me the next day. Same goes for your confidence: Sometimes you just need to charge it up so it's at 100 percent! Try these tricks and you'll be ready to take on the world.

1 Walk like a winner. Hold your head up high, shoulders back, big grin on your face. Posture was always super important in the dance studio, but it's equally important in life. Body language says so much! If you stand tall, you feel powerful and in control—and that's how people will see you.

2 Make a list of all your awesomeness. Write down everything you've accomplished—even the little stuff that makes you feel happy and proud. For example, "98 percent on my pre-algebra quiz; solo in the school choir; taught my dog how to stay, roll over, and shake paws." Then, when you're having a "downer" day, you can look at the list and remind yourself that you're pretty amazing and that there's a lot more of that to come.

3 Edit your self-image. Kind of like when you go on one of those photoshopping apps on your phone like Facetune and fix your red eyes or cover up a zit (not that I've ever done that, lol). You can just as easily adjust the way you think about yourself: See yourself as a winner, a leader, a go-getter, a doer. Erase all the other images in your mind that don't belong in that picture, then project it out there!

4 Ask an expert. If you want to be the best at something, you have to learn as much as you can about it from people who are the best. I knew I wanted to write my own music so it felt real and relatable to my audience, but I'd never done it before. So my friend's dad is a songwriter, and I asked him to work with me. I was really scared that first writing session; I stuttered and didn't know what to do or say. But the more he explained and talked me through the process, the more confident I felt. Whatever it is that you want to do or be, ask the right people questions and find a mentor who is willing to teach you what you need to know. When it came to dance, the older kids at the dance studio were always my mentors; I looked up to them and asked their advice.

5 Give back. This is a big thing in our family, and my mom always encourages us to volunteer and work with charities in any way we can. At Christmas, we'll load up carts of toys to donate to families who need them, and even when we were little, we were ambassadors for the Starlight Children's Foundation. Just recently we did a campaign for Dancers Against Cancer, and I plan on volunteering at the Vanderpump Dog Foundation in L.A. I'm also a founding member of Positively Social. It's about helping young people use social media in a positive way. It's more than just anti-bullying. It's also about presenting the best *you* online, so that you don't feel that every "like" matters or that what you see on social media is the real world. No matter what cause you choose, volunteering is a kind and generous thing you can do for others that also makes you feel great about yourself.

• •

BE UNIQUELY YOU

When I was younger, I always felt like I had to live up to people's expectations of me. I thought everyone was constantly
judging me, watching each move and tearing it apart, nit-
picking everything I did and laughing at me behind my
back. Some of the above was true—the competitive dance
world *and* reality TV can get a little crazy. But a lot of it was
my really active imagination and my lack of confidence. It
really got to me. Even when the criticizing stopped, I would
criticize myself. I remember standing in the wings at dance
competitions thinking someone from my team or another
team was *so* good that I couldn't possibly beat them—why
even try? Wow, that was a major problem! The minute you
start looking at others and thinking you're not as good, you
knock your confidence way, way down. And if that wasn't
bad enough, people were constantly comparing me to Maddie! My mom always begged people not to compare us; she
didn't think it was fair. And Maddie never once made me feel
I had to compare myself to her; it was more the dance world
and stuff people would say about us. Maybe you don't have
a sibling; maybe it's a girl on your soccer team or someone
in your class or scout troop about whom you just can't help
thinking, "If only I could be more like her!" Or maybe you

see Kendall Jenner or some other actress or supermodel on a magazine cover and think to yourself, "I wish I had her abs!" Wishing is one thing; obsessing is totally another. My mom always reminds me that no one is perfect and you can't know what someone else is going through; their life might not be as flawless and fabulous as you think. So when you're comparing yourself to them, you're not actually getting the whole picture—which makes it seem pretty silly and worthless, doesn't it?

It also takes the steam out of your dreams; I don't know about you, but I'm not really motivated to achieve my goals when all I can think about is, "Will I ever be as good as her?" My mom will always remind me that you have to celebrate your own achievements and victories, not get stuck thinking about someone else's and letting yourself feel overshadowed. So yeah, I happen to live with a sister who is ridiculously awesome and accomplished and good at practically *everything*, and that's impossible to overlook. But I don't compare myself to Maddie; instead, I feel inspired by all she does. She's my role model. She supports me and she pushes me to be the best Kenzie I can be—she inspires me to do more than I ever thought I could or would.

If you're going to compare yourself to someone, then make sure it's a positive force that pushes you forward—not a negative one that holds you back. We all need someone to look up to, but it should never make you feel jealous or loser-like. I also tell myself that comparison can't be a good thing; it puts the focus on the wrong person. Do you really want to be spending your time and energy on someone else's life instead of your own?

THE KENZIE QUIZ
WHAT DOES YOUR FAVE COLOR SAY ABOUT YOUR CONFIDENCE?

Personally, I'm all about quizzes—the ones you see on BuzzFeed and Wishbone or in teen magazines are my faves. I wanna learn which Disney princess I'm most like (I usually get Ariel, because I like to collect stuff, explore, and have fun), which *Riverdale* character is my soul mate (Jughead Jones!), and what my fave flavor of ice cream says about my personality. So did ya know that if you like cookie dough ice cream you're someone who does DIY projects at home and loves dogs? How accurate is that?

I've sprinkled several of my own quizzes throughout the book—answer as honestly as you can and then check each key below. You might just learn something about yourself!

1. **You will likely find me wearing red:**
   a. *Never. It's way too bright!*
   b. *On Valentine's Day only*
   c. *Head-to-toe in a cool new tracksuit*

2. **If I could paint my room any color it would be:**

   a. *Calming Cream*

   b. *Slate Blue*

   c. *Sunshiny Yellow*

3. **The color of my underwear is usually:**

   a. *White, off-white, or nude*

   b. *Navy or black*

   c. *Polka-dot, striped, or neon*

4. **If I could choose any baseball cap to wear it would be:**

   a. *White or gray with no words or logo on it*

   b. *Black or navy with my fave team's name*

   c. *Metallic gold or silver*

5. **My fave dance costume would be:**

   a. *A white or pink leotard*

   b. *A black crop top and hip-hop pants*

   c. *Red sequin booty shorts and a matching top*

If you answered mostly As: Your color choices show that you're someone who prefers to whisper instead of shout—that's okay, as long as you're not dulling your personal sparkle! But for fun, how about adding a pop of color to your outfit or room with a few small accessories, like a cute hot-pink clutch or some fuzzy orange throw pillows? A little brightness can boost your self-esteem big-time!

If you answered mostly Bs: Your fave hues reveal a person who's true blue: loyal and consistent with your thinking, which makes for an awesome friend and good student. Here's a thought: Why not switch things up a bit? A green hoodie today, a purple one tomorrow? Getting out of a rut will rev up your confidence!

If you answered mostly Cs: Your bright, showy color choices scream, "I've got self-esteem!" Yay for you! When you walk into a room, people can sense your power and confidence—they're hard to miss!

USE YOUR VOICE

Easy for me to say, right? I'm a singer and I never really stop talking! But like I said, in the beginning, especially when I was going into a recording studio and working with song-writers and record execs on my album, I was really scared to open my mouth. I was afraid they would think I was just a kid and I didn't belong, or that I had no idea what I was talking about and shouldn't speak unless spoken to. I thought they would laugh or, worse, completely ignore me. Maybe you've felt the same in a class or a club or even in a social situation with your friends: You want to say something, but the words won't come out. My mom always tells me how important it is to "assert myself." I had to ask what that meant, but now I totally get it: It means saying what you think and feel without being afraid. It's sharing your opinions because they're valu-able; it's showing the world you won't be pushed around, held back, or walked on like a doormat. I know we're just kids, but that doesn't mean we have to keep quiet when something is important to us. The world is going to be all ours one day, so we better start showing we have what it takes to be responsi-ble, smart, and *outspoken*.

If you're still tongue-tied, try these tips:

» Think about what you want to say before you say it. Have a plan and even a script scribbled down on a piece of paper—especially if it's for a class or a business situation. If you have no time to write out a speech, then at least rehearse it in your head for a few seconds.

» Consider what you want to happen when you speak up—what's the end goal? What do you want the reaction of the people listening to be? Do you want them to feel sad, mad, happy? For example, if I wanted to convince my teacher *not* to give us homework over a three-day weekend, I'd have a strategy all laid out before I said a peep. No matter how unfair I felt the situation was, I'd totally keep my cool so I wouldn't put her on the defense. I'd be really polite and respectful, and I'd remind her how hard the class worked all week. Then I'd throw in that she deserved a break, too! Think about how you can say things to get the results you want, and choose your words carefully—that can make all the difference.

» Don't just talk, listen. Sometimes we blurt things out without hearing a word someone else is saying. I know I'm totally guilty of this; I tend to get into these big, heated discussions with Maddie, where I'm all fired up and she just sits there, staring at me like I've lost my mind. Why? Because she's agreeing with me but I'm not listening! Oops! Before you say anything, make sure you know where others stand and what's going on.

» Timing is everything. If you want to speak up, find the right moment. Don't interrupt when someone is speaking (rude); don't shout when a room is quiet (double rude); don't wait till someone is really upset, tired, or hangry to bring things up (that's really asking for trouble!). Consider whether it's better to have a conversation one-on-one or in front of a group—does your statement really need a big audience? Could it wait till you are alone instead? I remember when I was really mad that my mom wouldn't let me ride in the front seat of our car—so unfair! I'm thirteen and just as tall as she is! I was frustrated, so I brought it up when she was exhausted, cranky, and seriously not in the mood. Yeah, that didn't go down very well. She dragged me with her to the police station to actually ask an officer if there were specific height/weight requirements for riding in the front. It turns out there are, and I didn't weigh enough (by like two pounds!). So Mom's answer was a stern "No!" I waited a week or two and tried again, this time on a bright sunny day when my whole family was together in L.A. feeling relaxed and happy. This time, things went better. Mom was smiling and laughing at one of Greg's silly jokes, and I saw my opening and took it: "So when we go to dinner tonight, can I ride in the front?" She rolled her eyes but then gave in: "Fine, fine. You win." Did you hear that? I won! And all because I found the perfect moment to plead my case. Couldn't have timed it better!

KENZIE'S CRAFT CORNER

INSTA-FABULOUS COASTERS

Since this chapter is about self-confidence, I thought
it would be really fun to celebrate yourself with a
coaster made out of a fave photo you posted to your
feed!

WHAT YOU'LL NEED:

* Mod Podge sealer
* A large paintbrush
* 4 x 4" white ceramic tile
* 4 x 4" photo of yourself (Shutterfly, Mpix,
    and InkDot all print Instagram
    pics)
* Small felt stick-on circles

1. *Start by painting a layer of Mod Podge on the tile. Press the photo onto the tile and let it sit about 5 minutes.*

2. *Now apply another layer over the photo. It will look white but dry clear—so don't freak out! Allow this layer to dry about 20 minutes.*

3. *Apply five more layers of Mod Podge over the photo; you can do fewer, but I wanted mine to be really waterproof so I could rest a mug on it. Let the layers dry overnight.*

4. *Apply the felt circles to the bottom of the tile on each corner. You can make a whole set of these to share or give as gifts. Personally, I love to use mine when I'm curled up on the couch drinking a cup of hot cocoa.*

ASK KENZIE

Since fans are always asking me questions, I thought I'd tackle a bunch in every chapter.

This girl in my school comes over to me every morning and says something really mean about my clothes, like "Your outfit is so extra." It makes me feel awful!

Okay, so clearly this girl is very jealous of your wardrobe—why else would she be constantly putting it and you down? You—or your sense of style—are a threat to her, so she is picking on you to knock your confidence down. I say rock your outfit! She doesn't have to like what you're wearing or think it's pretty or cool (I bet she secretly does). Everyone has their own taste and style; if not, we'd all be wearing the same dull uniform every day and look like Minions. I know it hurts when people bully or say mean things, but try to understand what's behind it: This girl really doesn't like herself very much. I also know it's tempting to insult her back, but my mom has always told me that it's a big waste of time and energy to engage with a bully. I would ignore her, but if you must say something, then tell her, "I'm sorry you feel that way," and walk away. Don't argue or try to defend your fashion choices; that's what she wants, to make you mad or sad or insecure. She's trying really hard to push your buttons! If you pay no attention to her, she'll eventually give up. Unfortunately, she'll probably move on to someone else (and you might wanna share this advice with them!).

I want to take this hip-hop class at my school, but I'm really scared I'm going to look ridiculous and embarrass myself.

I was always an acro dancer, and the first time I did lyrical group routine, I stuck out like a sore thumb. You can't let the fear of looking dumb hold you back. Everyone who tries something for the first time probably doesn't look great doing it. There's a learning curve, and the more you practice and take classes, the better you'll get at it. I think it's important to ask yourself why you want to take hip-hop. Is it because you love the music and think it would be a really cool thing to learn? Is it because you want a fun new way to exercise? Or maybe a lot of your friends are in the class and asked you to join in? All of the above should outweigh the fear factor. Don't put too much pressure on yourself to be perfect. If you can go in that dance studio thinking, "Yeah, whatever!" you'll do just fine—probably a lot better than you think. And, most important: You'll have a great time. So go for it!

My older brother is super smart and all the teachers in my middle school are always comparing me to him—especially when I don't do as well on a test. Why do I always have to be just Kenny's little sister?

Gee, I'm not familiar with this at all. Are you kidding? I was known for the longest time as Maddie Ziegler's little sister (okay, I still am!). On *Dance Moms*, they even made me do the same solo, "Cry," she did in the same costume—just so they could see how I stacked up! And yeah, it can be annoying, but it can also be a plus. It made me want to prove myself even more and pushed me to be a better performer and a better person. Maddie was a great example for me. Instead of feeling bad about it, can you find a way to let it motivate you? Don't blame your brother, either. It's not his fault that people put him on a pedestal. Find what makes you special and one-of-a-kind and show that to everyone, your teachers included. When you find it, no one will see you as a mini version of your brother ever again.

RULE 2
PRACTICE POSITIVITY

"THE GLASS OF MILK MAY BE HALF EMPTY— BUT IT GOES GREAT WITH COOKIES!"

I remember this time back in school in Pittsburgh: It was the fifth-grade farewell show, and I was in third grade. They actually let the younger kids attend that year, and I was trying to show off by doing some really hard dance moves. Of course, I slipped and fell on my butt. I remember sitting there on the gym floor, staring up into the faces of all these kids laughing hysterically at me. I could have cried or run away; I could have died of embarrassment. But instead I laughed right along with them. I laughed so hard, my cheeks hurt (the ones on my face, not just the ones I fell on!). And at that moment, I realized something: You can't control the situation, but you can control how you react to it. You always have a choice: You can go to the bright side or the dark side. Okay, maybe I sound a little like a *Star Wars* movie—but I mean it! You can pick positivity and own it.

I am a pretty positive person. My friends and family find this annoying at times, because when they're stressing out over something I'm all, "Yeah, it's fine! Relax!" I wasn't always this way. When I was younger, at the dance studio, I cried a lot and I let things get to me. I remember one time I was given a hip-hop solo against two of my teammates, and they were much better at this style of dance than I was. What did I do when Gianna asked me to rehearse it in front of our moms? I ran to the bathroom and bawled my eyes out. Looking back on it now, I wonder what the point of acting that way was. It didn't do anything to fix my fear that I was going to embarrass myself. It didn't make me a better dancer—it just caused drama. If I had to do it all over again, I would tell myself to suck it up. I would look at it more as a challenge and try to get myself excited and into it. But I didn't—and they aired it all on TV. Way to go!

Sometimes it's really tough in the moment not to feel sensitive or sad or negative—emotions can really sneak up on you, and they can be overwhelming. That day at the studio, mine felt like a huge tidal wave crashing over my head. But that's when you have to learn to push that positivity button!

KEEP YOUR EYES ON THE PRIZE

What is your goal, the thing that you really, truly want more than anything else? At the moment, I'd say mine is a sold-out stadium tour around the world. Or maybe a duet with Ariana Grande? When I was younger, I used to just go into a studio and record a track that someone else wrote the lyrics to. I dreamed of one day writing my own songs based on my own experiences—I'd even write down lyrics on my phone. I would say to myself, "One day, wait and see! I'm gonna do this!" Today, I keep song notes on my phone and add to them as a reminder *never* to give up—and guess what? They've become songs on my new album! When you're feeling discouraged, hold that prize out in front of you—see it and reach for it and let nothing stand in your way. It's like when my dog Maliboo doesn't feel like playing with me because she's being lazy; I could call her name till I'm blue in the face, and she ignores me. She wants to lie around all day on her little doggy bed and let me wait on her hand and foot (or in her case, paw and paw). So I get out one of her treats and I dangle it right in front of her nose. She immediately leaps up and snatches it out of my hand. The same goes for you: If you need something to motivate you out of a bad mood, then hold out that goal and jump for it!

BE GRATEFUL FOR ALL YOU'VE GOT

I went to Home Goods with Maddie and my mom to "autumn up" my room for fall and Thanksgiving (even though it was like eighty degrees in Pittsburgh in October, which is so bizarre!). I spotted this pillow—THANKFUL—and although I promised my mom I wouldn't get any more pillows for my bedroom (I have a gazillion), I couldn't pass it up. I think it's a great message, and it reminds me that I am so, so lucky to have everything I have going on in my life—especially my friends and family. Anytime you need a boost of feel-goodness (is that a word? Well, it should be!), remember all the amazing things you have in your life to be grateful for. You can even make a list, and don't leave out the small stuff: your dog that licks your face after you just ate a bowl of ice cream, the fact that you just finished your English homework (yay, me!), the Dunkin' Donuts drive-thru . . . You get the point. When I'm feeling thankful, I'm less likely to whine and complain (my mom is thankful for that!). My day is filled with so many more possibilities, and

I'm more creative, energetic, and open-minded. Gratitude is good for you and even better if you spread it around: When you say "thank you" to someone, they feel appreciated and loved, and that makes everyone get along a lot better in this world.

SMILE!

This seems like a no-brainer, right? It's hard to feel bad when you put on a goofy grin. I read somewhere that smiling actually sends a message to your brain: "Don't worry! Be happy!" So when you're feeling negative, the easy fix is to turn that frown upside down—and there are lots of good reasons why you should. First of all, you look better. I don't care how many pouty duck lips people post on Instagram, a bright smile is always prettier in a pic. Second, a smile is contagious: If you smile at someone, they usually can't resist smiling back at you—it's a reflex, like when the doctor hits your knee with that little hammer and your leg flies up. And finally, when you smile, it makes people think you're cool and confident. Whenever I'm worried about an interview, I walk into the room with the biggest smile on my face. Trust me: No one will ever know how nervous you are!

START SINGING

Or whistle. Or hum. Music is a major mood lifter—Maddie and I will break into the entire soundtrack of *High School Musical 2* in the back of the car. Why? Because when you sing "Fabulous" like Sharpay, you can't help but feel fabulous. There are actually a lot of really smart people who study "the science of singing" and say it's a legit way to brighten your day—even if you're totally off-key, like Maddie. Personally, I cannot *not* move when I'm singing; my body automatically vibes along. Which brings me to dance—another amazing way to make yourself more merry. I know this, because I've tried it with my BFF Lauren. We blast some music and jump up and down, waving our hands in the air like we just don't care. Every time, we wind up rolling on the floor cracking up because we both look so ridiculous. So there you have it: scientific proof that "dancing it out" makes you happier!

BOUNCIN' BACK

I'm not the best athlete, but I can dribble a ball—and that's how I see myself when it comes to facing a big letdown. You gotta *be* that ball and bounce. I really believe that disappointment makes you a stronger person. My friend Nina wanted to be a Rockette, and she tried out again and again and again—seven times in all. Each time they told her no, until the very last one. Well, you only need one yes—and she got it! And it means even more to her now, knowing how hard she worked to get to this place. Like I said, when something doesn't go your way, there isn't a lot you can do to change it—stuff just happens and sometimes you get knocked down. That's when you need to get back in the game!

I remember when I was nominated for a 2016 Teen Choice Award and I really wanted it *bad*. It was the first year Musical.ly was out, and they nominated me for Top Muser along with Loren Beech, Kristen Hancher, Ariana Renee, Jacob Sartorius, and Baby Ariel. It was such a cool award, and I wanted to be the very first to win it. When they called out the name of the winner—Baby Ariel—I was like, "Dang it!" For the record, she deserved it, because she's amazing and a really sweet girl. But still, it hurt and I threw myself a little pity party. I told myself that fans were the ones who decided this award, so that must mean that people didn't like me (or that they liked her more). Ouch. I tried my very best not to let it show on my face that whole night while people were interviewing me and taking my picture. But yeah, it felt like when they tighten your braces—a dull, constant ache.

That night, Justin Timberlake won the first-ever Teen

Choice Decade Award, and he said something really cool that got me thinking: "We all fall down, but what we do after that fall is what makes history." Now, I understand that it was just one award and that there will be others. You don't need a trophy (or in this case, a surfboard) to prove you're good enough. The point is, what do you do after the disappointment? What do you do (thanks, JT!) to make history?

For starters, you can let it make you more determined. When I was eleven, I went into this audition and I totally blew it. I forgot all my lines and I had known them when we left that morning for the casting call. I guess my nerves got the best of me or I was distracted or tired—whatever the reason, I knew I didn't do my best and that I wasn't getting that part. That was that. Normally, I wouldn't have cared, but this was a role I really wanted based on a book I had read and loved. On the way home in the car I pouted and refused to talk. I was so mad and so disappointed in myself, and I could feel those emotions eating me up inside.

"Kenzie, there'll be other movies and other roles," my mom assured me. "It happens. You'll get the next one or the one after that. Or something better will come along. Things happen for a reason."

At the time, I didn't want to hear it. I didn't want to believe that anything good could actually come from this. I didn't want to be told, "You win some, you lose some." What was good about losing a part I was so perfect for? I let myself feel bad—my mom called it "wallowing." So yeah, I wallowed, but only for a little while. I gave myself that one night to feel bad; then I put it behind me. This was just one audition; it wasn't the end of my entire career. The next day was filled with possibilities and new things to go for; I didn't have time to mope—I had work to do. And that became one of my rules: When you're disappointed or angry at yourself, it's okay to feel those feelings. But just like Elsa sings in *Frozen*, you gotta "let it go!"

Another time, toward the beginning of our Day & Night tour, I was onstage with Johnny Orlando and my voice did this weird thing. I cracked on a note during "Day & Night"; then I was so embarrassed, I messed up the lyric. My heart started pounding: Had the audience noticed? Did they think I was terrible? Did Johnny notice? Did *he* think I was terrible? I looked out into the faces of the fans and everyone was smiling, singing along, and having a great time—it didn't seem to bother them. Then I looked over at Johnny and he was totally doing his thing. When I asked him about it later, he was like, "What note? What are you talking about? You're crazy—you killed it." So the whole thing had really been in my head; I built it up as this huge disaster when it wasn't anything like that. I remember thinking, "Wow, Mackenzie, you can really blow things out of proportion!" and it was a good lesson to learn. Almost always, the things we think are *really* bad just seem that way in the moment. Come tomorrow, they will mean nothing and everyone will forget all about it. You create the drama yourself when there isn't any, and, like my friend Lauren would say, "that's just so extra!" Who needs it?

I wish there was a way to instantly wipe away all disappointments—like a giant pink eraser! That way, you'd forget them and they wouldn't linger in the back of your mind, poking at you and reminding you that you messed up/failed/didn't get what you so badly wanted. I don't have an eraser big enough to do that, but I do have some ideas to help you let go of a letdown. . . .

DISTRACT YOURSELF

If your brain is busy, you won't wallow. Some people read; others knit. Me? I give myself permission to watch one of my fave shows on Netflix. It takes me to a happier, crazier place. I just watched the entire first season of *Riverdale* and I'm obsessed, especially with Betty and Jughead, aka "Bughead" (if Cole Sprouse and I were a couple on the show, we would be "Mughead," just sayin'). Anytime I want to feel better about my life, I just tune in to see what these teens have to deal with: murder, lies, parents in jail. After an hour or two, I'm like, "What do I have to complain about? I feel so much better!"

My other favorite distraction is YouTube, especially conspiracy theory guy Shane Dawson. Lauren and I like to watch him, although he does freak us out. Even the way he talks is spooky—really low, sometimes in a whisper, and he gets close to the screen so you're staring into the whites of his eyes. We're afraid to blink or we'll miss something really important—like his theories on aliens and unsolved mysteries or what happens when you play a Britney Spears or Taylor Swift song backward (there are all kinds of weird, hidden messages!). I totally believe what he says now; it makes perfect sense. My only word of caution: Do not watch these videos alone or after dark if you scare easy. Lauren and I ran screaming into her brother's room the other night. We had to watch a happy video about cute baby animals just so we could calm down and go to sleep!

BELIEVE SOMETHING BETTER IS OUT THERE

My mom always says, "When one door closes, another opens." As much as I hate to admit it, she's right! Whenever I've lost out on something, another opportunity—usually something much bigger and better—has come along, and I'm actually relieved that the first one wound up not working out. It takes a little faith, not just in yourself but in the universe, that stuff happens for a reason. If I think back now to when I was a competitive dancer, all I wanted to do was win; it was my life and anything less than first place was a big disappointment. If I didn't take home the top prize, it felt like the end of the world. But now I have so much more going on, new opportunities to be creative, to make music, to write this book—you name it. Maybe if I had won more, I wouldn't have left that life, and I'd still be competing. Then where would I be? In a room filled with trophies instead of on tour around the world doing what I love the most! But I never knew that back then. I didn't have this crystal ball that could look into the future and say, "Kenzie, don't worry about it! You're going to be playing to standing-room-only crowds in the UK!" You may not be able to see your future either, but trust me when I say that one setback (or a bunch) isn't going to define who you are. There's more, more, more in store!

NO REGRETS

This is a big rule for me: You should never be sorry you gave something a shot and it didn't work out. My mom says that mistakes and failures are really life lessons and the stuff that shapes us. I remember when I was six, a friend asked me to a sleepover at her house and I wanted to go *bad*—all the cool girls were going. But I couldn't; I had dance. It was pretty much my answer to every party, playdate, after-school activity, you name it: "Sorry, I have dance." I started to regret not being a "real kid" with a real life. I didn't like missing out; I felt like I had no childhood, and it made me sad and angry. But fast-forward seven years, and I see how those times I had to say no and give up stuff got me to where I am today. If I had to do it over, I'd make the same choices—and I probably wouldn't whine and complain about them as much. My stepdad, Greg, says, "You make your bed, you lie in it." That's what this is all about: You make your choices because you believe they're the right ones for you, and you deal with what comes with them. Instead of moping, try and see what the "takeaway" is.

It's like when you read a book in English class and the teacher asks you, "What does the author want you to take away from the story?" What's the message and the bigger picture here? In my case, it was "hard work pays off." I know that now, even if six-year-old Kenzie couldn't see it and was throwing a tantrum because she couldn't go to a pizza party after school. I see the value in all those hours I put in at the dance studio, because it taught me about dedication, discipline, and never giving up. And if I was grumpy back then, it's because I was really little and hadn't yet realized that regrets are a big waste of time and energy. And okay, I really liked pizza. . . .

BREAK IT DOWN

I don't know about you, but when I'm disappointed, it feels like there's peanut butter in my brain: It's all kind of a sticky mess until I sit down, analyze honestly what happened, and try not to blame myself or someone else (sorry, Mom!) for causing it. It may not be fun to revisit, so give it a little time. Then, when you're ready, ask yourself, "What went wrong here? What *really* happened? What can I learn from this?" I promise that when you break it down, any disappointment seems a lot less humongous and heartbreaking. Also, consider whether your goals were realistic: I mean, did I *really* stand a chance of beating Baby Ariel out for Top Muser? Probably not. Once you figure things out (which is like wrestling with a tough algebra equation), you'll feel much better. Just dealing with my disappointment rather than hiding from it gives me a sense of accomplishment. I can check it off and move on.

KENZIE'S CRAFT CORNER

DIY CRAYON CANDLES

Candles help me relax at the end of a tough day. I love to light them in my room: They smell amazing, and staring at the flickering flame is soooo soothing. You can choose colors that match your room décor or the season (e.g., red, green, and white for Christmas). Make sure you have an adult supervise when you're working with hot wax.

WHAT YOU'LL NEED:

* *Old broken crayons in different bright colors*
* *Dixie cups (small paper ones)*

* Candle wax (the smokeless soy kind they sell in
   flakes is best; you can find it on Amazon or in most
   craft stores)
* Essential oils in your fave scents (I find lavender very
   relaxing)
* Candle wicks (the ones with a metal circle on the
   bottom so it stands up easily)
* Popsicle sticks (for stirring)
* Heatproof glass containers to pour wax into (I like
   mason jars or small juice glasses)

1. Start by peeling the paper off your crayons; if you
   soak them in water for a minute or two, the labels
   will come off a lot easier. Now break the crayons
   up into small pieces.
2. Fill a Dixie cup 2/3 full with candle wax and place
   crumbles from a single-color crayon on top.
3. Microwave for 2 minutes, then at 30-second
   intervals, until all the wax is completely melted
   (careful not to burn!).
4. Add a few drops of essential oil and stir with a
   Popsicle stick.

5. Now you're ready to pour your first layer of colored wax into a mason jar. You want to place the candle wick in the center of the wax so it will set (you can also rest two Popsicle sticks on the rim of the container and secure the wick between them to hold it upright between fillings).

6. Wait until the wax is completely hardened—about 20-30 minutes—to pour the next layer.

7. Repeat with several other crayon colors, each in a different cup, building rainbow layers of wax in each jar until your candle reaches nearly to the top rim. I do about three or four different colors in mine, depending on the size of the jar/glass.

8. Trim the wick so it's about ½-inch long.

9. Now light your candle and chill!

ASK KENZIE

I'm completely devastated! My BFF just got the lead in the school play and I have a lame part in the ensemble. I know I should be happy for her, but I'm so miserable for myself!

What's more important to you: a starring role or your friendship? That's what you need to ask yourself, because if you keep acting "miserable," your friend is going to think you blame—or, worse, hate—her. I know not getting a big part is disappointing; there were plenty of times I had to dance in the back while other girls on my team took the featured roles in our group routines. And there were even more times that my sister got a solo in a competition and I didn't. So I know how you're feeling, like you're stuck in the middle of a tug-of-war. One side of you wants to be happy and supportive of your friend because her hard work paid off. But the other side of you says, "Hey, just a second! I worked my butt off, too!" Tell your BFF that you're happy for her and so proud of her. Do the right thing and be a good friend. Remind yourself that there will be other plays, other parts, other opportunities to be in the spotlight, and you want your BFF to be happy for you when it's your turn. My dance teachers always used to tell us, "There are no small parts, only small dancers." So be a big person: Shine in whatever role you're playing and pitch in to make the production a huge success. Now *that's* star quality!

I just took my math midterm—I was sure I did really well, but when I got it back, I'd made so many careless mistakes, and I got a C+! I have never gotten such a bad grade in my life and I don't know what to do!

Start by taking a deep breath and stop freaking out. It's one grade, one test. You know there will be other tests the rest of the year, so you can build your average back up. Learn from this experience so it doesn't happen again: What went wrong? Did you forget to study something in your notes? Did you run out of time and not get a chance to double-check your work? One time on a big homework assignment, I did an entire equation perfectly—except I wrote one wrong number, so the entire answer was incorrect. Oopsie! I would try and talk to your teacher and your parents so you can figure out why you made mistakes. I'm sure that with a little effort, you will do much better next time. Just don't beat yourself up about it—these things happen to all of us! Ask your teacher if there's something you can do to earn extra credit: Even if there isn't, he/she will appreciate that you want to do your best.

I really want to adopt a dog, but my parents say no way. I saw the cutest little puppy at a shelter and my heart is breaking that they won't let me bring her home!

I have been pestering my mom night and day to let me get a second dog—a little brother for Maliboo! I saw one I fell in love with, and I literally went on Instagram Live begging her to let me take him home. But since my mom's the one who has to feed our Maltipoo princess, walk her, and take care of her most of the time (okay, maybe all of the time), the answer was a pretty definite NO WAY. So it's clear I have to prove to her that I am willing to pitch in a lot more. Then maybe she'll believe that I can handle not just one but *two* dogs. So what is making your parents say no to you? Do they think you won't do your share of caring for a pet? Is where you live not pet-friendly or big enough for a dog to run around? Get to the heart of the issue instead of just being heartbroken—hear your parents out, and don't yell, cry, or tell them they're being mean and unreasonable. Trust me, I've tried all of the above and none of these methods work! Show your mom and dad that you can be calm, cool, and respectful of their wishes and concerns. Maybe they will eventually cave in. In the meantime, why not volunteer at a pet shelter where you can play with lots of adorable dogs that need your love and attention? It's my happy place!

A DAY IN THE LIFE OF

MALIBOO

Since I was probably old enough to talk, I begged, pleaded, and, okay, tried to bribe my parents to get me a dog. Then, four years ago at Christmastime, Maliboo came into our lives! I can't even begin to tell you how excited I was to get this teeny-tiny fluff ball of white fur. She's truly become a member of our family—definitely the most spoiled member—and we all love her so much. Greg is kind of the "alpha," the one Maliboo listens to the most, because when we were away shooting *Dance Moms*, he raised her from the time she was a baby. Maliboo gets majorly pampered! No dog food for her—she eats scrambled eggs for breakfast, and fresh salmon, chicken breast, and squash or edamame for the rest of her meals. She eats on a plate beside everyone at the dinner table and she has very good table manners! Every year on her birthday, we take her to Dairy Queen for ice cream.

Maliboo's also quite the fashionista. She loves dressing up (Greg just told my mom the other day she needs some new sweaters, lol!) and posing for pictures. I have full-on photo sessions and she will vogue for the camera. She travels everywhere with us: She was on the movie set with Maddie, and she's logged trips to Texas, New York, and California (always flying first class, of course, in her own seat). My mom will literally take her shopping at the mall. While my mom is trying on clothes in a dressing room, Maliboo will just lie there on the floor at her feet.

I'm the one who taught her tricks: "sit" and "lie down," and she's been working on "shake paw," though she's not quite mastered that one yet. It's more like, "I'll raise my paw an inch if you give me a treat." She hides her bones everywhere. She puts them wherever she wants, and we sometimes find them in the weirdest places, like up the stairs or between blankets in the closet. When we're back home in our Pittsburgh house, she runs to check that they're where she left them and never forgets her hiding spots.

She sleeps in bed with my mom and Greg, and wakes him up at least once a night to go outside. My mom is very happy that Maliboo's considerate enough to bug Greg and let her sleep!

I give her baths and blowouts, but Greg usually finishes because she squirms and gets me soaking wet. She's a handful, but the love of our lives.

RULE 3
BE A LEADER, NOT JUST A FOLLOWER

"DON'T SIT DOWN WHEN YOU CAN STAND UP."

During the second season of *Dance Moms*, I changed elementary schools in the middle of the year. I wasn't too worried about it—I thought I would make friends easily. But I found myself a target, mostly because people assumed they knew me from TV. There was a lot of whispering behind my back and some pretty cold stares. I remember being at recess, and this girl walked up to me: "Just because you're on a TV show doesn't mean you're the coolest kid here—so don't go thinking you are." I was shocked; I didn't know what to say! I wasn't trying to act cool; I wasn't asking for any special treatment. She was totally judging me, and I didn't even know her!

I walked away; I was kind of intimidated, because it came out of nowhere and I was so *not* the person she was accusing me of being. Eventually, I made some friends, but the crazy thing is, this happened more than six years ago, and I can still remember it like it was yesterday. I know these were just words, but some people use words as weapons, and they can hurt you if you let them. They can make you feel small; they can make you feel invisible; they can make you see flaws in yourself that don't even exist.

That wasn't the last time I was bullied. As I got older, the rudeness wasn't shouted in my face; it was posted on my social media. People would be so cruel to me in comments: They would compare me to my sister, saying that I wasn't as pretty or as talented as Maddie. They called me fat; they said I was ugly and had big bunny teeth that stuck out. They made fun of my costumes and my routines, called me a crybaby and a loser. People even hacked my Instagram to make me look bad! I felt like I was constantly being attacked, and I hadn't done anything to cause it. It made me paranoid and insecure. Before I posted a photo, I'd ask my friends, "Do I look ugly in this picture? Do I look skinny in this picture?" I was always second-guessing myself, worrying what someone might write, and dreading every time I scrolled my feed for comments. I remember when Maddie was away on the Sia tour, I cried and cried over stuff that was happening online—and I felt like she was so far away and I needed her help. She called one night and she could hear it in my voice: "Kenzie, what's wrong?" I guess I wasn't my usual perky self. I told her that I was sad and overwhelmed by all the hate—why were they picking on me? What had I done to cause all of this?

"Nothing. You've done nothing," Maddie reminded me. "They're jealous and they're trying to take you down. Don't let the haters get to you. Block them from your social media and out of your head."

Having my family and friends stand behind me was what made it all shift and get better—it felt so good to tell someone! I took Maddie's advice and I told myself that these "trolls" have nothing better to do with their time than pick on someone who's trying to live her dreams. How sad and pathetic is that? I can see now that these people are strangers to me, no different than the girl who told me off at recess—they don't know what they're talking about, because they don't have a clue who I am inside. I take social media very seriously—I always think before I post, and I know that I have a responsibility to be a role model and be careful what I say, because millions of people (literally!) are reading or watching. But not everyone thinks this way; some people just post to get a reaction, to make someone feel bad or make themselves feel more important. They hide behind their laptop or phone. That's the scary part of what our generation has to deal with. If you're going to be on Instagram, YouTube, Twitter, or Facebook, you have to understand that what you say matters and that it's very hard to take it back once you put it out there! Someone has seen it—probably lots of someones—and it's like lighting a match. You don't know how big a fire that can start.

It took a while, but I've finally reached a place where I'm happy with who I am and how I look and dress, and no one can take that away from me. Honestly? I don't care what people comment anymore. I have a much tougher skin, maybe because of what I went through, or maybe because it makes me feel stronger that I'm talking about it and not letting the haters win. When you stand up, it takes the power out of the bullies' hands and puts it in yours. So many fans tell me, "I was bullied, too!" when they hear about my experience. So none of us are alone in this—we have each other! My song "Monsters" is about the feelings I had, and I think it's the best advice I can give anyone dealing with haters:

"Don't believe everything they say / And be yourself at the end of the day. / Don't let anyone stand in your way."

TAKE A STAND

My mom is someone who believes you don't just "talk the talk—you walk the walk." I remember the first time she said it, I scratched my head and asked what the heck that meant! I wasn't walking or talking at the time (I think I was actually sitting in the car, listening to my music), so it didn't make a lot of sense. But now I get it: Don't just say you believe in something, put actions behind it. Be an example of what you stand for in your life. Maybe it's easier to keep quiet (and that's what bullies count on), but that's like giving up. You shouldn't just stand up for yourself; you should stand up for others who are powerless. If you see something bad going on and you do nothing about it, doesn't that make you just as guilty? Using your voice is the only way people will learn what needs to change. It's a step in the right direction. So whatever you're thinking and feeling, whatever makes you upset or angry because it's just not right, don't hold back! Yeah, I tend to blurt stuff out (sometimes just to embarrass my sister), but I'm someone who thinks you should always say what needs to be said. You are you—one of a kind with your own mind! I know a lot of adults think kids should be seen and not heard, but I think the opposite: We're entitled to our opinions, and we have some really good ones. Just remember, when you speak up:

» **Be honest.** No one can hold it against you if you speak from your heart. Be genuine, and explain why you feel what you feel, and why this matters to you, big-time. If there's a problem, offer some ideas of what can be done to fix it. Which brings me to . . .

» **Always have a plan.** Complaining is never a solution; action is. Even the smallest step you take can bring about a positive change. For example, when I heard there were so many homeless dogs on the streets and in shelters, it made me so upset! Seriously, I wanted to cry every time I thought about it, and I felt really helpless. My mom sat down with me and we agreed I had to do something ASAP. My closet was getting crowded, so I decided to sell some of my clothes on Poshmark to benefit an organization that helps dogs find loving families. My mom made me understand that if you're passionate about something, you can't just sit back and expect other people to do all the work. You have to do your part as well and get creative with ways you can pitch in.

» **Be nice.** I hate when people yell at me—it's something that always bothered me when I was at my dance studio. So I try to remember that when I plan on making a point myself. If you're very emotional about a subject, you may feel like shouting. Don't; it doesn't help people hear you any better. It's probably a good idea to take a breath, walk around the block for a while, and think about what you're going to say before you say it. It's not even a bad idea to try it out on a friend first—role-play so you can figure out how to get a positive reaction in real life. Take it from me: Kindness is key.

» **Don't play the blame game.** When you accuse someone, they usually shut down or get defensive. I know this, because that's how I feel when Maddie accuses me of taking her clothes and (shocker!) I actually didn't. I get really, really defensive, and it erupts into a screaming match ("Did not!" "Did too!") and my mom has to step in and break it up. A better way to handle it: Never assume or accuse—even if you're pretty sure you're right. When you speak up, make it about the problem, not who you think is causing it. So note to Maddie: Next time your shirt goes missing, try asking, "Has anyone seen it?" instead of saying, "Kenzie, I'm going to kill you!" I might actually help you look for it!

THE KENZIE QUIZ
SAY WHAT?

When faced with a frustrating situation, how would you handle it? Be honest.

Situation 1: Your fave dessert place is going to start closing early—no more late-night cookie runs when you need them! You call the owner up and say:

A. *"OMG! I can't believe that you're closing Dessertz-R-Us at 5 p.m. every night! This is horrible and inconsiderate—not to mention really dumb! I'm gonna tell all my friends to stop going to your store because clearly you don't care about your customers!"*

B. *"I was so disappointed to hear you won't be delivering past 5 p.m. I love your chocolate chip cookies, and my friends and I order them every time we need to cram for tests—it gets us through late-night study sessions. Maybe you could do some later deliveries just during midterms and finals weeks? My friends and I could definitely spread the word and make sure it's worth keeping the store open a few extra hours."*

Situation 2: Your social studies teacher gives you a low grade on your oral report. You stay after class and tell her:

A. "Are you kidding me? My report was totally worthy of an A! It was amazing and brilliant. Anyone can see that—why can't you?"

B. "I feel really bad about the grade I got on my oral report. I worked very hard on it, and I would appreciate it if you could explain to me where I went wrong so I don't make the same mistakes again. Is there anything I can do to improve my grade?"

Situation 3: Your BFF cancels brunch plans on you last-minute—for the third week in a row. You text her:

A. "Seriously? This is so not cool. This is the last time I'm asking you to go anywhere. You clearly don't care about being my friend, so I won't bother being yours."

B. "Is everything okay? I've noticed that you've had to reschedule the past few weeks, and I miss hanging out with you. Please let me know what's going on."

Situation 4: Your hairstylist gives you a haircut—but it's not the mirror image of the photo you showed her of Kendall Jenner. You say:

A. *"Are you blind? Does this look anything like the picture? I am not paying a cent for this horrible haircut, and now I'm going on Yelp to write a bad review!"*

B. *"Um, maybe there was a misunderstanding: It's not exactly the look I was going for. Can we do something to fix it so I love how it looks on me?"*

Situation 5: Your mom promised that when you turned thirteen, you'd be allowed to go out with your friends by yourselves. It's been a month since your b-day, and she still hasn't let you. You tell her:

A. *"Mom, you are so unfair! You lied to me! You broke your promise! I'm a big girl and you need to trust me and get over the fact that I am growing up!"*

B. *"Mom, can we talk about something that's been bothering me? Remember when you said I could go to the mall with my friends? Well, I've been patiently waiting. I'm ready and I'll be really responsible. Can we give it a try?"*

If you chose mostly As: Hmm, you can get a little hotheaded when something or someone annoys you. I get it, but maybe there's a better way to get your way than throwing a tantrum. Try patience and politeness, and don't point a finger (even if someone is clearly to blame). My mom always says you catch more flies with honey.

If you chose mostly Bs: *Yesss!* You're really good at making your point without making a scene. I'm impressed! You understand that being calm, cool, and considerate is the best way to make friends and influence people.

ASK KENZIE

My school has a no-phone policy during the day and I think it's so wrong! What can I do about it?

Why do you think it's "so wrong"? That's where you should start. Why do kids need phones during the day? To feel safe in case of an emergency? To be able to text or call parents and friends and make plans? To find out more info on a subject? To listen to tunes that calm you down when you're stressing before a test? All great reasons! Then consider where your school administration is coming from: What do they *not* like about cell phones in the classroom? They distract you from your work; they allow kids to cyberbully or look at inappropriate stuff online; they prevent kids from connecting face-to-face. Um, also great reasons. So make two lists: one pro and one con, so you understand both sides. When you've done all your research, make an appointment with your school principal or assistant principal (the person who sets the school rules) to discuss it. Make sure you come prepared to talk—not fight—and understand that you may not win this time. But at least you've shared your feelings and have spoken up for your classmates who feel the same. You've given the administration a lot to think about, and things might just change down the road.

My parents have two totally different sets of rules for my older brother and me and it drives me crazy! I get better grades and I'm more responsible, but they let him do *anything* he wants because he's fifteen and I'm thirteen!

Maddie and I are a little more than a year apart, and I totally see that my parents treat her differently. I will always be "the baby" in their eyes, and it's impossible to convince them otherwise. So I hear ya. I feel like my sister always got to do stuff before I did. When Maddie was thirteen, she went to the Grove in L.A. with her friends, on their own. But now I'm the same age, and my mom still insists that an adult has to tag along with us. No matter how much I argue that it's not fair, she insists, "Maddie is more responsible." I don't think so. I just think it's because she's the older one. That comes with a VIP card! But I know that I get away with a lot of things, too. My mom tends to excuse or "spoil" me more than she would Maddie, because I'm the younger one. For example, sometimes when I leave my towel on the bathroom floor (oops!) my mom will pick it up, but she won't tolerate that from my sister, who should "know better." And if I ask her for a snack, she will make it for me so I don't miss a second of the TV show I'm watching, while I've heard her say to my sister, "You know where the fridge is." You should talk to your parents and tell them you feel like there is some unequal treatment going on and give some good, clear examples. But just remember what it may bring: more responsibility for you. Sometimes being the baby is a bonus!

RULE 4
GET YOUR BODY MOVING

"GIRLS NEVER SWEAT—WE GLOW!"

That alone should be reason enough for us to exercise, right? What girl doesn't want to be gorgeously glowy? I mean, I'm always applying highlighter to my cheeks—and when you exercise, you get an all-natural shine! That said, I could probably do more working out every day. I used to do Pilates and I loved SoulCycle—the Bieber vs. Beyoncé class was amazing. Recently, I even took a hot yoga class with Johnny and Lauren's mom in Toronto. It was like a hundred degrees in the room, but the instructor was so positive. She made melting fun and relaxing.

You've probably heard from your PE teacher, your coach, or your dance instructors that it's smart to exercise. Teenagers especially need to get their bodies moving every single day. Why, you ask? Well, let me tell ya, because my choreographer/ fitness role model Rumer Noel has taught me a thing or two about the subject:

» **It's good for the mind as well as for the body.** So there are these cool chemicals called endorphins that can make you feel peaceful and happy. When you exercise, your body makes them in your brain, which is a good thing. They're great for relieving stress (and teens have a lot of that), even for helping you sleep better at night. Rumer says it's the same feel-good vibe you get from eating chocolate—minus the calories. Another plus: When you work out, you can actually afford to eat more chocolate. So win-win!

» **It makes you look better.** Besides the glow I mentioned, exercise keeps your body at a healthy weight and makes you look more fit and toned. I definitely notice a difference when I've been dancing a lot to prepare for tour: My arms and legs look more muscular from all the hard work I put in. Exercise takes you from flab to fab!

» **It gives you a sense of "yay me!"** How awesome and accomplished do you feel after you've put in a tough workout? I may be tired, but I feel like someone should put a gold medal around my neck. My confidence and self-esteem soar!

» **You'll be healthier in the future.** I know you're probably not too worried at the moment about health risks when you're older. You probably just hear your parents complain about them—so you know down the road you'll have to deal with them as well. Exercising now when you're young can help lower the risk of scary stuff that adults get, like heart disease, high blood pressure, osteoporosis (weakening of the bones), even diabetes. Also, the habits you set for yourself at a young age carry into your adult life. Rumer says do it now; your body will thank you later.

There are different types of exercise—and I don't just mean spin class vs. kickboxing. The exercise that gets your body revved up (heart pumping, blood flowing) is called "aerobic." Rumer makes a point of telling me how dance is an aerobic powerhouse. You know it's working if you start breathing hard (or, in my case, I collapse on the floor, panting like my puppy!); your heart is doing its job and delivering oxygen to all parts of your body. I think of it like Postmates: We deliver! Tweens and teens need about an hour of aerobic activity every day, so if you're on a dance or sports team, you're probably getting enough. Skiing, rollerblading, swimming, biking, jogging, bouncing on a trampoline—all of these activities are awesome as well. Sometimes I'll take Maliboo out and we'll speed-walk. There are lots of huge hills in my L.A. neighborhood, and she'll run along to keep up with me (her legs are a little shorter than mine). Eventually, I wind up carrying her—which is like speed-walking with a five-pound weight! I know a lot of kids who view exercise as a chore, but I try to always make it fun and switch it up so it's not boring. I'm someone who bores easily, so I can't do the same thing every day or I'll lose interest. Gotta stay motivated!

• •

5 COOL WAYS TO MAKE FITNESS FUN

I am all about F-U-N, so if I'm going to exercise, it has to be something that makes me forget that what I'm doing is actually good for me. If you hate the idea of exercise, don't think of it as a chore. Think of it as a cool activity or adventure—something to do with friends, post on your Instagram story, or distract you from doing your homework.

Trapeze: While you fly through the air, you're actually working your upper and lower body as well as your core. Hanging from a swing and *not* letting go requires some serious arm and shoulder strength! Look for circus arts classes for tweens and teens that teach you how to use the trapeze, hoops, and silks.

Hula-Hooping: I was obsessed with this when I was little—how long can you keep the hoop up on your hips without letting it drop? Did you know this playground game tones your thighs, abs, butt, and waist? And check out the new weighted hoops—they burn two hundred calories in thirty minutes. That's like five Oreo cookies right there!

Fencing: If you like the idea of playing action hero and getting to wave a pointy sword in the air, check out this workout. Lots of places offer fencing classes for kids that are safe, challenging, and fast-paced. Fencing gets your heart rate up and tones your arms and butt (those lunges are like doing squats, but so much more fun when you yell, "En garde!").

TurnBoard: I love mine! I asked my mom to get me one for Christmas one year, and my sister and I were obsessed from the minute we hopped on. It helps you gain balance and coordination and perfect your pirouette. My turns have improved so much since I've been using it. To keep turning, you have to engage your core, butt, and leg muscles. You can get my official one at www.balletisfun.com.

Dance Dance Revolution: Who says video games aren't good for you? I know a lot of kids who get a group of friends together after school to play this on their game system—it's so much fun to challenge each other by busting some moves! You'll need the console, game, and dance pad to get started. The idea is to dance in sync with a song on the screen—and you'll burn as many as eight calories a minute as you do!

LET'S KICK IT!

One of the few people I trust as a trainer is Rumer. She does all my choreo for my tour, and she's given me some amazing stretches and DIY exercises I can do on the road or in my dressing room. She's the reason I'm not panting onstage after a show!

NOTE: Make sure that before you start any health/exercise program, you check with your parents and your doctor first.

RUMER'S RULES

»   **Junk the junk food.** "Sugar and junk food, as yummy as they are, do nothing great for your body. They just make you feel bloated and have energy crashes, and eventually creep into unwanted places on your body. There are good sugars, though! Fruits and sweet potatoes (complex carbs) are good energy you can put into your body before exercising. These slowly release into your bloodstream and don't spike blood sugar levels. If you're looking for other healthy snacks to munch on, try apples and almond butter (good sugars, vitamins, and protein); almonds or trail mix (protein); bananas (muscle function); high-protein/low-sugar protein bars; and carrot or cucumber sticks with hummus (vitamins and protein)."

» **Drink up!** "You must stay hydrated, especially when dancing and sweating it all out! For girls/women, you need about eight glasses of water a day. Maybe even a bit more if you are super active that day. Water is extremely important for your muscle function as well. Your muscles will dehydrate and tighten up with not enough hydration."

» **Make a promise to move—every day.** No sitting around like a couch potato! "If you can't take a dance class or get to the gym, there are plenty of other fun activities you can do. Combine aerobics with flexibility and strength training (see exercises on the next page) and eating right, and you'll be in great shape!"

Photo courtesy of author

Hello world!

Photo courtesy of author

My best friend since day one!

Wasn't I a cutie?!

I don't know how my mom got me to sit still for
this photo! Or the bunny for that matter!

I was on the move from day one.

Just bein' goofy.

Raawwrrr! So ferocious!

My mom LOVED putting me and Maddie in matching outfits.

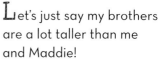

Let's just say my brothers are a lot taller than me and Maddie!

Kid's Choice is always a blast with the girls.

One of my first award shows. I was so excited!

Photo courtesy of Jen Lowery Photo

Family photo.

Me and Brookie Cookie doing the duck face!

I NEVER dress for boys!

So proud of my sister. At the *Leap!* premiere.

Cheesin' with KyKy.

Maddie and me playing the biggest game of Twister!

Sometimes it's nice to take a break from work and just focus on being a goofy kid!

Me and Maliboo at the beach.

Jessa and me chilling by the Christmas tree. ♥

I can always count on Maddie to be by my side.

A scary but fun night at Knott's Scary Farm.

Photo courtesy of Glenn Nutley

. . . and sometimes
on my back!

Photo courtesy of author

Strolling along Hollywood's Walk of Fame

One of my many photoshoots with my guncle Glenn Nutley!

• •

RUMER'S "READY-SET-SHAPE UP!" PLAN

THE 5-MINUTE UP-AND-AT-'EM

"Do this every morning before school to get your brain and body revved for the day! Even if you're running late, you can always find five minutes, right? Choose your favorite song that gets you hyped up (how about Kenzie's 'Breathe'?). Then try these exercises to quickly warm up your whole body."

1 Start jogging in place for about 30 seconds, just getting your blood moving.

2 Add high knees. Do 16 of them regular; then add another 8, throwing your arms up in the air on the last count. Do these enhanced sets of 8 twice.

3 Lunges in place. Keep your upper body straight, with your shoulders back and relaxed, chin up. Step forward with one leg, lowering your hips until both knees are bent at about a 90-degree angle. Make sure your front knee is directly above your ankle, and make sure your other knee doesn't touch the floor. Hold for a few seconds, then push back up to stand. Do this 10 times with each leg.

4 Squats. Stand with your feet slightly wider than your hips. Your toes should be pointed slightly out, and you want to pick a spot on the wall to stare at to help you keep your balance. Hold your hands straight out in front of you and sit back and down like you're sinking into an imaginary chair. Keep your head facing forward as your upper body bends forward a bit. Try not to round your back, and keep your thighs as parallel to the floor as possible, with your knees over your ankles. Press your weight back into your heels, hold for a few seconds, then return to starting position. Do this 10 times, rest, repeat.

5 Add a Kenzie Kick! Once you're standing up between each squat, lift your right leg out to the side, squeezing your butt muscles tight. Repeat with the left leg on the next squat and continue alternating.

• •

THE KENZIE KRUNCH

"Kenz is about fun, but she knows that you gotta work hard to play hard! Just by adding this 10-minute exercise routine into your day, you will start seeing major results (hello, abs!). And this workout's a ball—a yoga ball, that is!"

» **Exercise 1:** Grab a large yoga physioball. Lie back on the ball so your lower back is touching the ball—that way, you get a full-body crunch. Crunch for 20 reps and make sure you squeeze your abs. They will help you stay balanced and not fall off!

» **Exercise 2:** Now flip over. We're going to do a plank for 20 seconds on the ball. Kneel and rest your elbows on the ball and come up into a push-up position, abs tight and back straight. Use your elbows to roll the ball in a circular motion, clockwise and then counterclockwise, as if you were stirring a pot. Do 10 total and repeat.

» **Exercise 3:** Hold the plank while bringing your knees one at a time toward the ball, like you're "kicking" it. Do 10 on each side. Make sure you don't knee the physioball too hard without stabilizing yourself, or you will face-plant!

» **Exercise 4:** Remove the ball. Time to do mountain climbers for 20 steps with alternating legs. Start in a plank position. Keep your abs pulled in and your body straight. Squeeze your glutes (butt muscles) and pull your shoulders away from your ears. Now pull your right knee into your chest, tightening your abs. Quickly switch and pull the left knee in. At the same time you push your right leg back, pull your left knee into your chest. Continue to switch knees, right, left, right, left, so that you are doing a "running" motion. Count 20 switches, then rest 20-30 seconds and repeat.

DANCERS' "GET DOWN" STRETCHES

"These are great for making you more flexible and achieving those long, lean dancers' lines."

LEGS AND HIPS

» Stand with legs slightly wider than hips' width apart. From here, bend your knees into a grand plié second position, using your hands to push your knees outward pointing toward your toes. You can straighten your left arm and push your left shoulder forward to stretch out your left hip, then repeat with the right hip.

» From that position, rotate hips to the right into a right-leg lunge, with hands flat on the floor on either side of your leg. Hold for about 15 seconds, letting your body weight stretch you. Breathe! Tuck your head into your chest, and stretch your legs straight, keeping both sets of toes pointing to the right side, and place both hands flat on the floor on either side of your right leg, with your upper body relaxing over your leg. Do a couple of inhales and exhales here.

» Come back down to lunge, but this time bring both elbows down to the floor in front of your right leg to stretch in a deeper lunge, keeping your back leg straight.

» Place your back leg (your left leg) flat on the floor with your butt tucked under and place both hands on top of your right knee, stretching your left hip. From that position, place your left hand on the ground and, using your right arm, reach up toward the ceiling and then back toward your left foot to grab it and pull toward you gently. Hold for about 10 seconds. Tuck and sit flat on the floor and hug your right leg into your chest. After you stay here for about another 10 seconds, come back into your right-side lunge, transfer your weight into a left-leg lunge, and repeat on your left side.

ARMS AND SHOULDERS

» Pull your right arm across your body; inhale and exhale. Now take your right arm down and up and over your back, pulling your elbow down to your back with your left hand. Breathe in and out again. Repeat on the left side.

BACK AND NECK

» Stand with your feet hips'-width distance apart. Bend forward, placing hands flat on the floor, knees as straight as you can. Stretch! While hanging over, use your arms to pull your head closer to your chest.

» Now grab your elbows and slowly rock your upper body from side to side about 8 times.

» Place hands flat on the floor again, and bend legs to begin to plié and roll up through your back *slowly* (count down from 8), returning to standing and leaving your head to roll up last.

» Once up, take your right arm up toward the ceiling to reach up and over on the left side of your head. Gently pull your head over to the right side and take a few breaths here. Do the same with stretching your head up and over to the left side.

» Drop your head and roll it around in a circle twice to the right and twice to the left. Your neck should now feel nice and loose!

. . . .

10 TUNES THAT
GET ME MOVING

1. *"Wolves" by Selena Gomez and Marshmello*
2. *"New Rules" by Dua Lipa*
3. *"OMG" by Camila Cabello*
4. *"Make You Mad" by Fifth Harmony*
5. *"What Lovers Do" by Maroon 5 featuring SZA*
6. *"Love So Soft" by Kelly Clarkson*
7. *"Silence" by Marshmello featuring Khalid*
8. *"Friends" by Justin Bieber*
9. *"Distraction" by Kehlani*
10. *"Confident" by Demi Lovato*

. . . .

YOU ARE WHAT YOU EAT

This is what Johnny and Lauren's mom, Meredith, always tells me—which is why the Orlando house (my home away from home) is stocked with low-sugar, low-fat, high-protein options—hummus, green juice, fruit, veggies, SmartPop!, you name it. I love how Meredith always takes a recipe and reworks it so it's healthier. For example, when she grills BBQ burgers, she'll use half lean ground beef and half turkey meat—and it's really delicious. She's also big on chickpeas (Lauren's fave and full of protein) and snack kits that you can eat on the run because we're always going somewhere: cheese and crackers, cut-up apples, veggies and dip. She also gets us into the great outdoors by hiking—we just did the "Tree of Life" hike to the HOLLYWOOD sign, and it was a great workout and so Instagram-worthy! If it weren't for Meredith, I'd be a couch potato sitting around snacking on Doritos all day (with two very happy helpers)! I asked her to share some of her recipes for my favorite Orlando-family meals.

BREAKFAST SMOOTHIE

Johnny and Lauren's mom whips this up for us in the a.m. or as a snack in a to-go cup if we're about to hit the road. It's like a healthy version of a strawberry milkshake!

Ingredients:

* 2 c. frozen whole strawberries
* ¾ c. frozen blueberries
* 1 medium banana, fresh
* 2 c. skim milk

Place all the ingredients in a blender and blend until smooth.

GOBBLE-'EM-UP TACOS

Serves 2–3

Instead of beef, these tacos are made from lean ground turkey meat, which makes them healthier.

Ingredients:

* 1 ½ T chili powder
* 2 tsp. ground cumin
* 1 tsp. ground paprika
* 1 tsp. salt
* ½ tsp. garlic powder
* ½ tsp. onion powder
* ½ tsp. dried oregano
* ¼ tsp. cayenne pepper
* 1 lb. ground turkey
* Taco shells and all the "fixins'" to top the tacos:
  shredded cheese, lettuce, chopped onion, and
  tomato

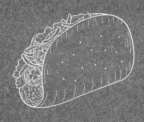

1. In a small bowl, mix all the spices and salt
   together.
2. In a large nonstick skillet over medium heat, cook
   the turkey meat, breaking up clumps with a wooden
   spoon or spatula, and stirring until no longer pink.
3. Stir in the spices. Reduce heat and simmer,
   stirring occasionally, until most of the liquid has
   been absorbed.
4. Heat your taco shells in a toaster or the oven then
   fill with meat. Top with anything you like.

GOOD-4-U
CHICKEN FINGERS

Serves 2.
Double the recipe if you're having a crowd or party.

Ingredients:

* ½ c. flour
* Salt and pepper
* 1 egg
* 1 T milk
* 1 c. plain or seasoned bread crumbs
* 1 package chicken tenders (about 6 pieces)
* Nonstick cooking spray

You'll also need:

* 3 shallow dishes

1. Preheat the oven to 425 degrees. Line a cookie sheet with tinfoil and spray with cooking spray.
2. Place the flour in a bowl and season with a pinch of salt and pepper. Beat the egg and milk

together in a second bowl. Pour the bread crumbs into the third bowl.

3. Dip the chicken tenders first into the egg, then the flour, then the bread crumbs—kind of like in an assembly line.

4. Now place the breaded chicken tenders on the cookie sheet and bake in the oven for 12–15 minutes, until crispy golden brown.

KENZIE'S CRAFT CORNER

SUPER-EASY OMBRÉ SNEAKERS

WHAT YOU'LL NEED:

* Painter's tape
* A pair of white canvas sneakers, lace-ups or slip-ons—your choice. They can be old or new.
* Old newspapers
* Rit fabric dye in a single color
* Small spray bottle

1. Use painter's tape to cover the rubber trim and sole of the sneakers—basically anywhere there isn't canvas.

2. Stuff both sneakers with a sheet of newspaper so

the color doesn't "bleed through" when you paint. If your sneakers have laces, remove them. Cover your workspace with newspaper as well, so you don't make a huge mess!

3. Pour some dye into the spray bottle, about one-eighth of the way up—a little goes a long way. Add water to fill to the top and shake.

4. Spray the front of the sneaker starting at the toes with your color mixture—about one-third of the shoe.

5. Now pour out half of the liquid in the spray bottle and add more water to fill to the top. You want to create a "watered-down" color that's lighter than the first one you made. Shake.

6. Spray the middle section of the sneaker. The color should be slightly lighter.

7. Pour out half of the liquid in the spray bottle and add water again, filling to the top. Shake. This should be the lightest color.

8. Spray the heel of the shoe to finish your ombré look. Let the sneakers dry overnight before putting in the laces and wearing.

ASK KENZIE

I sprained my ankle and now I have to sit out of soccer practice and use crutches for the next six weeks! I feel like a slug not being able to exercise!

Okay, so maybe your feet and legs are off-limits; that doesn't mean you can't do some great arm exercises! One of my faves is a bicep curl that you can do with or without 1- or 2-pound weights. Rumer says to do this 60 times: "Sit with your arms out to either side of your body, elbows bent and even with your shoulders. Tense your arm muscles, extending your arms out, then bring them back up to start."

I know I'm supposed to drink water during the day, but I just think it tastes so bland and boring! Any ideas?

I love infusing water with fruit—it makes it taste so much better! All you need is a pitcher or large jar—about 2 quarts is a good size. You can add oranges, lemons, limes, pineapple, watermelon, strawberries, raspberries—or even a combo of a few. Cut them up, give a stir, and let them soak. Mint also tastes really refreshing. Put on a lid and you can keep them in the fridge for about three days. You can even find infuser water bottles that you can take with you to the gym or dance studio.

My ballet shoes stink! Any tips on how to freshen them up?

Dancers and stinky feet go hand in hand (or is that foot and foot?). The best solution is not to wear the same pair day after day; rotate two pairs so they have a chance to dry out and breathe between classes. If that's not an option, there are a lot of things dancers do to get the odor out: Let them sit in the sun (UV rays and fresh air work wonders); put them in a plastic bag in the freezer (it eliminates the bacteria that causes the stink); sprinkle them with baking soda, then place in a paper bag for 24 to 48 hours (soaks up the bad smell); spray two paper towels with vinegar and stuff in each shoe for 3 to 4 hours (neutralizes and speeds drying). I also like to keep sneaker balls in mine when they're in my dance bag—it prevents serious stink from building up.

RULE 5
EMBRACE YOUR STYLE

"MINE IS DEFINITELY ALL ME—EXCEPT FOR
A FEW THINGS I MIGHT HAVE BORROWED
FROM MY SISTER'S CLOSET."

Yes, I admit it—I might have nabbed some stuff out of Maddie's closet when she wasn't looking. It's just so tempting, because we like the same stores and brands, and she hardly ever notices unless I happen to be out with her and forget where my wardrobe came from (oopsie!). Then I get yelled at—a lot. "Kenzie, that is my hoodie, not yours. Give it!" It's honestly the best part of being sisters who are so close in age, height, and size—I have double the amount of clothes to choose from right under my roof! It's like going to the mall—but it's all free! Then my mom comes into the picture: She "borrows" from Maddie, too! I swear the other day I saw her leaving the house in one of Maddie's dresses from her fashion line and I was like, "Oooh! I'm telling!" We agreed not to rat each other out and just keep sneaking stuff out of Maddie's closet when she's not looking! It's just so much easier that way. Why ask? She'll only say no. She's very possessive of her clothes, and she thinks if she actually lends me something, she'll never see it again. And she might be right about that. . . .

I have a lot of thoughts on style—I've even designed a line of activewear for Justice stores. I think as a tween/teen you should always be comfy—anything too short, too tight, too revealing is going to make you self-conscious. I think it's important to look your age—not your mom's. I don't like anything itchy/scratchy or stiff. I have to be able to move and, more important, *lounge* in whatever I'm wearing. If I can't sit crisscross applesauce on my couch or kick my feet up on my bed wearing it, it's not for me. I'm definitely a sporty girl who loves sweats and sneakers, but I think over the past few years, my style has been evolving. I like it to have a bit of an "edge," and reflect the fact that I'm in music. Maddie will tell me sometimes that I look very "rock and roll," and I take that as a compliment. I save the dresses and fancy stuff for the red carpet, and that's because you're being photographed by a gazillion paparazzi. If it's just me hanging out with my friends, I am dressed down in jean shorts and a cropped tee.

I have a passion for fashion that feels good. I like pastels like light blue and baby pink, never bright colors or neon. Here in L.A. they have this amazing outdoor shopping mall called the Grove. There's a Brandy Melville, Topshop, Zara, all in one place, with a cute trolley car that runs between the stores—it's like I died and went to shopping heaven. But with so many possibilities, I've had to create my own fashion rules: For starters, only wear what suits you, your life, your personality. Be yourself—not someone else. Although I would love to raid Zendaya's closet (she's the coolest!), I would still only borrow clothes that feel like Mackenzie, not like someone else. Unless of course it's Halloween, in which case YOLO!

I also don't believe you have to wear just one brand or deck yourself out all the time in fancy designer labels. Just because something has a name on it doesn't make it worth blowing all your babysitting money on. My sister, maybe because she's a little older, drools over pointy designer heels—shoes are her thing. Not me. I don't care how "status-y" they are—if they crunch my toes and make my feet hurt, they're not worth it. And those cute little clutches she carries on the red carpet? Yeah, I definitely need something bigger, because I always have a ton of stuff to tote around with me!

• •

WHAT'S IN MY BAG?

Um, how about everything but the kitchen sink? I seriously do pack everything into my mini backpack. Like a Girl Scout, I like to be prepared.

* A planner that I don't really use—but, ya know, just in case! I usually keep my calendar on my phone.
* A journal. I write down song ideas/lyrics, feelings, and sometimes what I did during the day so I don't forget.
* My phone. I go nowhere without it. If I don't have it on me, my fingers get twitchy!
* A phone charger—because I always run my battery down since I'm on my phone so much!
* A portable charger. Nice in concept, but I forget to charge it and it's always dead when I need it. Oops.
* Cough drops for when I go onstage and my throat is

sore or dry. I had a cold a few months ago and now I'm fine, but I keep 'em handy.

* Advil, because I always have headaches. Somehow, if I carry them in my purse it wards off a headache. If I forget them, I'm literally begging my mom to go to the drugstore ASAP.

* Colored pencils. 'Cause I love to doodle and scribble.

* A bag filled with makeup for touch-ups: lip balm, mascara, blush, eyebrow pencil. Anything that will help me create a fast face if I need it.

* My wallet. I usually have some cash, but I also have my own debit card in there. You never know when you might see some cute outfit in a store window or a souvenir at the airport that you *have* to have. I know not every teen has this in her purse, and I feel really lucky that I do.

* Moisturizer, for face and body. I'll sit on a plane or even in the back of a car slathering it on.

* Headphones, so I can listen to my tunes and tune out the world around me.

* Hair elastics/scrunchies. If it's hot, I want my hair up. If it's a bad-hair day, I want my hair up. If I'm bored and tired, I want my hair up. No wonder there are so many floating around at the bottom of my bag....

* Receipts, ticket stubs, some random slips of paper that I have no idea what they are, gum wrappers...

* Sometimes my laptop—but only if I'm going to be out for a while or on the road or I have an important assignment to do (like writing my book!). Otherwise, it takes up way too much room!

* Extra clothing. The other day—I am not kidding—I found a spare pair of socks, and I have no idea how they got there! I might throw in a thin sweater or hoodie if I'm going somewhere that's air-conditioned and don't feel like carrying it. Or maybe I'll toss in an outfit to change into after working out with my trainer.

MY PERSONAL STYLE FILE

You should know that finding your signature style doesn't happen overnight: You have to go through a lot of trial and error and fashion "don'ts" till you figure it out. In elementary school, I was a walking disaster, probably because I let my mom pick out my outfits for me. I wore a lot of pink and sparkles and stuff with unicorns and smiley faces. And dresses! One day I was in a dress and I had gym class, so they made me sit out so I wouldn't flash everyone my underwear. Slowly, I started to figure out that I wasn't a glitter girl: I liked my clothes a little more laid-back. I asked Maddie's advice, and I started reading fashion magazines and trying on stuff in stores. A picture took shape in my mind: *This is my style; this isn't.* And now it's so much easier. I know instinctively if something will or won't look good on me, and I can put together an outfit in seconds because a lot of my tops and bottoms are in the same color family. Of course, this isn't to say that I don't occasionally stray from my fashion philosophy. Maddie's boyfriend was visiting recently and he and I decided, as a joke, to buy matching pairs of Crocs. I literally have not worn those shoes since second grade—I used to deck them out in all those fancy Jibbitz jewels! Maddie was positively horrified, but we thought it was funny—and I have to admit, they're pretty comfy. You bounce when you walk!

My final style rule is super important: Don't try too hard. Don't pile on the accessories, overdo the hair and makeup, wear things that are over-the-top for the occasion or place you're going. For example, a faux-fur coat when you're going bowling or false eyelashes and red lipstick to school are a bit much. You know you're trying too hard when you look in the mirror and you can't see *you*; all you see is the outfit or the hair/makeup, and not the person underneath. If that's the case, take off something—or a couple of somethings—until the real you shines through.

MACKENZIE'S MUST-HAVES: WHAT A GIRL NEEDS IN HER CLOSET

I probably own a gazillion T-shirts and dozens of pairs of sneakers, so narrowing down my list of my absolute necessities was a tough one! Maddie describes my style as "sassy and carefree." I think it's just "me" and I truly dress for whatever mood I'm in. If it's a sunny day and I'm feeling really good about myself, I'll put on some fun accessories—like a choker, cute booties, and a cap. A lazy day puts me more in the mood for joggers and a tee—and my hair in a messy bun. Use my picks as a guide; your clothes should reflect your style personality (not mine, not your BFF's, not your mom's). That said, here are the entries in my Fashion Hall of Fame:

1 A white cropped tee: You can't beat a super-soft cotton tee. I pair them with anything, from a skirt to jeans to under a romper. It's the one basic you should have in your closet—I have about a dozen, because I wear mine so often!

2 A lived-in jean jacket: Mine is distressed with lots of tears and fraying, and I think that looks cool—edgy and relaxed at the same time. You can wear it with just about anything, from a sundress, to shorts, to a jumpsuit. Denim goes with everything. If you want to personalize it, you can add a few cute pins to one pocket or even use fabric paint to design an original masterpiece.

3 Flowy shorts—maybe some with a ruffled edge. You just pull them on and they're so comfy. Also, there's something a little flirty and feminine about them, so they make me feel pretty even if I'm dressing down for the day.

4 Denim shorts. Again, a staple of my L.A. wardrobe. Not too long, not too short, just right. I like them in all different shades of denim, too: everything from white to washed-out to dark rinse. Every time I see a cute pair in a store, I have to get them—even though I know I already have way too many.

5 A cropped hoodie. Simple and practical—I put mine on if there's a chill in the air—but the shorter, boxier shape is more fun than your basic zip-up sweatshirt. Look for colors like black, white, and gray that work with everything else you own. Or go for a bold color if you want to add some pop to an all-black outfit.

6 A two-piece set. I have these great velvet leggings that came with a matching cropped pullover and I love the look. It feels really put-together without much effort, and velvet makes anything seem dressier. I wear this all the time to go out to dinner. I'd recommend a basic black set in your wardrobe, but maybe also one in a bright color—so you can mix and match them. Velvet or velour feels very luxe.

7 A cute romper. Maddie and I have this inside joke about rompers: Every time we're going out and can't figure out what to wear, my mom says, "Oh, just put on a cute romper." So yeah, I do have a bunch that I like. Rompers are a little easier to wear than a dress; you can bend over and not worry that your skirt is too short! That said, they make going to the bathroom a little more complicated! But I still love the look, especially if it has interesting details, like lace, ruffles, or a cutout back. You can dress them up or dress them down; I think it's a teen's answer to the LBD (little black dress): the LCR—little cute romper!

8 A great pair of ripped jeans. I like them ripped at the knees and sometimes down the entire leg; I don't think I own any jeans that don't have rips in them. If I did, I probably made rips in them! It's just a trendy look that you can pair with anything, from a sweater to a blazer. I've been wearing them a lot on tour with vintage tees, and lately ones that reflect the city we're in—like a Pittsburgh Steelers jersey. My rule for jeans is simple: You have to be able to sit, bend, and squat in them. If you can't, ditch that denim.

9 A two-piece skort set. Again, it's all about ease: You don't have to hunt through your closet to find a top that goes with your skirt if it already comes with one! I love a cami in a cute print like floral or gingham with a matching wrap skort. For casual days, wear it with sneakers; for going out, a bootie or a wedge sandal. I think it's a lot more fun than a skirt/shirt option and has a playful, youthful feel.

10 Vans sneakers. Obsessed. I have a collection, and whenever a new color or pattern comes out, I'm begging to buy it. High-tops, low-tops—I never can say no. I think when you find sneakers that are super comfy to dance and run around in, you never wanna take them off.

11 Chokers. This short style of necklace gives your outfit a little edge. My favorites are velvet with a tiny charm attached. I keep them small and delicate so I don't overpower my look. I might even layer some chain chokers with a longer necklace to create a little sparkle if my top is too plain. You can mix and match gold, silver, and rose gold and different chain weights and charms. Have fun with it!

12 Baseball caps. Not just your fave sports team hat! Think cute fabrics, colors, and textures, like velvet, faux fur, leather, suede, and even metallic. They just add a little attitude to an everyday look. Messy hair? Don't care! I've got the cutest cap!

13 A pair of black booties—open or closed toe, preferably with a wedge or chunky heel. I wear mine with dresses, skirts, joggers—they honestly look cool with all of the above. I'm also short, so I love to wear a heel—it makes me walk taller—and in a wedge, I won't wobble.

14 My friendship bracelets: I never take them off! My fans made them for me and gave them to me at my concerts. People kept asking if I was dating a guy named Trevi because I wear one with that name on it all the time.

Sorry to disappoint, but he's the guy who made it for me—not my BF. I'm just super sentimental about all of them.

STORING YOUR STUFF

When it comes to your clothes, you need to be super organized: You can't wear it if you can't find it. So make sure your closet, your drawers, your jewelry box, everything that holds your wardrobe and accessories, is easy to navigate without Google Maps!

» Keep your faves front and center. The clothes buried in the back of my closet I will probably never wear; it's like the black hole of my wardrobe. If you love it, make sure you can see it and reach it.

» Fold your shirts like you work at the Gap. There's nothing worse than wanting to wear something and it comes out of your shelf wrinkled and rolled up in a ball (my bad!). And my stepdad, Greg, is *not* going to iron it for me last-minute (well, maybe if I ask really nicely).

» Hang and stack colors together (black with black, white with white, etc.). It makes it so much easier to find a certain shirt or sweater—you just go to the pink pile!

» If you have a "look" you love, then put that outfit together on one hanger (a shirt, a skirt, a jacket, a hat) so you don't have to hunt for individual pieces.

» Edit your closet every six months to a year. That means if you haven't worn something in that time, donate it to Goodwill, give it to a friend, sell it on Poshmark. It makes room for new stuff, which means a shopping spree!

» Create a shelf/drawer/bin just for bags, hats, scarves, gloves, sunglasses—whatever you collect and have a lot of. Don't just dump them on your dresser top or toss them over a hanger. My mom calls it "giving them a home." If they have a specific space, they won't disappear.

» Keep your jewelry from getting jumbled: An earring tree or jewelry box prevents you from losing earring backs and tangling chains. I just got a second piercing

in each ear, and I'm obsessed with keeping my earrings organized so I have lots of choices.

» Shoes should be stored where you can see them—not
in a messy pile under your bed. I hate searching fran-
tically for the left sneaker when I've already laced up
the right one! A simple shoe tree or clear boxes keeps
pairs together.

» Still stumped? A store like Bed Bath & Beyond, IKEA,
or the Container Store offers you lots of cool ways to
store your stuff. Look for baskets, boxes, drawer sep-
arators, multitasking hangers, even hooks to hang on
the back of a door. When Maddie and I were younger,
we used every inch of our rooms to store our clothes
and costumes—the closets were literally busting open
because we would just stuff our stuff in there! You can
make the most out of whatever size room you have, as
long as it's neat and tidy. (Just don't tell my mom I said
that, or she'll make me clean my room!)

KENZIE'S CRAFT CORNER

DIY BELT/SCARF HANGER

WHAT YOU'LL NEED:

* *Plastic hanger*
* *Assorted rolls of ribbon (narrow width, and different colors or patterns; you're going to wrap the rings and hanger with it)*
* *Hot-glue gun*
* *12–20 plastic shower curtain rings*

1. *Start by wrapping the bottom of your hanger in ribbon. You'll need a dot of hot glue to attach*

one side of the ribbon before you wind it around the plastic. When you have it all covered, cut and secure the end of the ribbon down with glue before doing the sides and hook on top.

2. Now it's time to wrap the rings! You can use as many as you want and even arrange them into a triangular pattern (eight across on top, then six; then four; then two). If you want to keep it simple, do two rows of eight. I guess it depends on how much stuff you have to hang! Wrap each ring in ribbon; you can alternate colors and patterns, whatever you think is pretty. Like you did on the hanger, start with a dot of hot glue to stick one end of the ribbon to the plastic; wrap, cut, and secure with glue at the other end. Do for each of the rings and allow them to dry.

3. Now it's time to attach the rings together. You can do this in a lot of different ways: by tying a small piece of ribbon with a knot; by using a zip tie; or by taking what I think is the prettiest approach: Cut a small piece of ribbon to tightly hold the rings together, trim, and hot-glue it.

You want to attach the rings to each other both horizontally and vertically. Allow all to dry for at least 20 minutes before the next step.

4. Now you want to attach your rings to the bottom of the hanger. Whatever method you used to secure the rings to each other, use to tie the top of your longest row of rings to the bottom of the hanger. When all is secure and dry, fill the rings with scarves, belts, bandanas—whatever needs hangin'! I think this looks so pretty, you can store it on the outside of your closet or even your bedroom doorknob. Instant art!

GETTING GLAM

I've learned a lot of tricks and tips from Maddie. Lauren and I will also watch hours and hours of YouTube makeup tutorials—especially the crazy ones where they make themselves look like famous people or aliens. These styles for hair and face are a lot easier and simpler, the basics you need to look your best every day.

FIVE 5-MINUTE (OR FASTER!) HAIR LOOKS . . . BY MY PERSONAL HAIRSTYLIST, MADDIE!

I love to torture my sister by making her do my hair all the time. She groans and complains, but I know she really likes to. It's her fault; she's used me as her guinea pig for her style how-tos on YouTube, and proved she's a pro. So of course I'm going to ask her to do it again! Don't tell her, but I've mastered these five looks, so now I can do them on myself in minutes. Next time when we make a video, maybe Maddie can be the model and I can be the one doing the 'dos!

All you need:

A brush and a few hair ties—the covered-elastic type are the best because they don't yank your hair when you try and take them out!

THE BALLERINA HALF UPDO

Use a brush to section hair just behind the ears. Comb back the top section and combine with the sides. Now grab the hair with your hands (it looks like you're making a ponytail), twisting it clockwise to form a loose bun at the crown of your head. Use the hair tie to secure the base of the bun—no bobby pins needed; you want it to have a messy feel. Once the bun is in place, pull a few "baby hair" strands out around your face—this looks really soft and pretty. Use your hands to fluff the rest of your hair (Maddie calls this "adding texture"). That's it!

THE FRENCH BRAID TOPKNOT

Start by parting your hair on the side—whichever side it naturally tends to go (for me, that's the left). Now you're going to do a French braid across the crown across the

right side—it's just like a regular braid, but you keep adding in small sections of hair from the outside. Secure the
braid once it's about the length of the top of your ear; the
hair tie will do the trick. Now scoop all the rest of your hair
into a ponytail, leaving the braid out. Use another hair tie
to secure the pony. Once you've done that, it's time to add
the braid in! Use yet another tie to make that happen. Don't
make the ties too tight; the look is kinda loose and messy;
you can even pull the braid out a little so it doesn't look so
uptight! When the braid is part of the pony, it's time to make
the topknot: Twist the tail into a bun and secure it with one
more tie. Pull a few tendrils loose around the sides and
you're all good to go. I love how this style *looks* complicated
but really isn't.

TEASED PONY (MINUS THE TEASING COMB AND PRODUCT!)

Scoop hair up in a high pony—and don't worry if it's not perfectly smooth. Bumps are actually okay, because this is a carefree, high-volume style (so sez my sister, but TBH I think she
was just in a rush). Fasten with a tie at the top of the head,
then use fingers to slightly loosen the crown and "fluff" out
the sides of the pony. Done and done!

DOUBLE TWIST

Part hair on one side where it naturally parts. Separate out a section of hair just above the ear about two inches wide on one side. Twist the section back and use a hair tie to hold it while you work on the opposite side. (FYI, if it unravels a bit, that's okay. You can retwist it tighter later or leave it loose.) Repeat sectioning on the other side, but now you're going to twist that section of hair back till you reach the ends. Now you're going to use a hair tie to secure the twists at the back of your head about halfway down (the tails are not twisted, just the sides). The remaining hair you left down can do anything you like: It can be smooth, it can be wavy, it can be crimped or curled. I just like how this look gets the hair out of my face and feels a little fancy.

DOUBLE DUTCH BRAIDS

My go-to hair style—it looks super cute and you can totally dance in it, work out in it, etc., without it coming undone. It's also a style that Kim Kardashian wears a lot (so you know it's cool). Part the hair down the middle. Use a hair tie to separate out one side section—you'll save that for later. Take a small section at the front of the loose section and start doing an "inside out" three-strand French braid. Basically, a Dutch braid is just a French braid you create by crossing the hair you add *under* instead of over each time. Continue braiding backward till you get to the very bottom and secure with a tie. Now do the other side the same way. This one may take a little practice, but it's so worth it; once you get the hang of it, it will be the one look you want to wear every single day!

FRESH FACE IN A FLASH!

I'm always in a rush to be somewhere *fast*, so I've had to streamline my makeup routine. When you're a teen, you really don't need a ton of makeup, and it should never take you more than ten minutes to apply. If it does, you're probably wearing way too much. You can always layer on more for a party or for going out, but for daytime and school, keep it clean and simple. When I look back at pics from my competition days and see how much makeup I wore (red lips! Smoky eyes! Heavy contour!), I cringe!

1 Always moisturize before putting on your makeup. Look for a light, everyday moisturizer that is "noncomedogenic." Translation: It won't clog your pores and make you break out. Moisturizer gives you a smooth base for your makeup and prevents it from going all cakey on you. Don't forget to moisturize your neck, too (that's a Maddie tip)—that way you won't get wrinkles there when you're older. Use your hands to blend the moisturizer in well and massage it in so your skin drinks it up.

2 Fill in brows. I like a brow liner that has a brush on the end. Brush your brow hairs up, then use the pencil to fill in sparse areas with light, feathery strokes. If you do too harsh a line, you'll wind up looking like Oscar the Grouch! Then use the brush side again to blend and shape. Finally, I set them in place with a brow gel so they don't get all crazy during the day.

3 Dot on concealer: a few spots under each eye; a few across the forehead, the tip of your nose, and the tip of your chin; and finally anywhere you have a zit that needs covering up. I like to use the kind that comes with a sponge-tip applicator; it just makes it easier to use it sparingly. You can use a brush or a beauty blender to blend it in, rubbing some into your cheeks, lids, and brow bone so it acts as a primer. Make sure you do a really good job on your blending; you don't want your color to look streaky.

4 Time to get glowing! I like a light bronzer applied to my cheekbones rather than a blush; it's more natural-looking. Maddie taught me how to apply it in a "backward 3" shape that skims across your temples, hairline, and jawbone. If I wanted a deeper color for a night look, I would add blush, contour, and highlighter. Highlighter is kind of my thing; I just scored this great palette of highlighters that are "holographic"—they kind of shimmer in shades of pink, lavender, and blue.

5 Use a big fluffy brush to apply a translucent powder to set all your makeup in place and minimize shine. Go lightly with the product; you don't want to put on too much or too heavy a powder or you'll look like you're wearing a mask. Let your natural skin shine through.

6 On to the eyes! I'm kind of obsessed at the moment with this peachy palette: The warm colors look so natural and really great on everyone, and they smell really good. I use a shadow brush to apply a light peachy shade across the whole lid, brow bone, and crease—this serves as a base. Then I add a touch of a frostier color to the inner lids and a darker one in the crease. Blend, blend, blend! Go back and add the frosty color to your brow bone for a bit of a highlight. If I was going out, I would probably add a dark brown shade with a liner brush along the upper and lower lash lines for definition—but for every day, it's not necessary. Blend, blend, blend (I know I sound like a broken record, but it's so important!).

7 A lash curler is your BFF. Seriously, I don't know how I ever wore mascara without curling first; it makes a humongous difference. At first you might be a little freaked out using a tool that grabs and clamps your lashes, but you get used to it. Have someone (your mom, your older sister, a pro at a makeup counter) show you how to do it the first time. Once your lashes are curled, apply a thin coat of mascara to the upper lashes. I find a thinner brush doesn't clump as much, but that's just me; Maddie tends to like thicker because it gives you volume. You find a mascara that's your fave through a lot of trial and error; some made me look like I had spiders on my face, others were too wimpy. Go to a place like Sephora or a department store and try on a few before you buy.

8 I like a sheer nude-pink lip tint or stain with built-in moisturizer; matte lips tend to look and feel really dry on me. You can find tints in a tube with sunscreen and treatment built right in, so not only does it look pretty, it's good for your lips, too. Apply and then press your lips together lightly to blend. I toss mine in my purse to reapply during the day, especially after I've eaten or sipped my caramel Frappuccino through a straw.

9 Your final step is to spritz your face with a setting spray; you wouldn't want your hard work to go to waste and your makeup to fade, would you? Let it dry for a few seconds, then grab your stuff and go!

KENZIE'S CRAFT CORNER

DIY MAKEUP BRUSH HOLDER

I love this "hack" that recycles empty toilet paper tubes into a cute, displayable holder to store your beauty tools!

WHAT YOU'LL NEED:

* 6–8 empty cardboard toilet paper tubes
* Scissors
* Large piece of stiff white cardboard
* A pencil
* White acrylic paint
* A paintbrush
* Some cute printed or patterned paper (the
    kind you find in the scrapbook
    section)
* Hot-glue gun (ask an adult
    to help you)

1. Start by figuring out how you want to arrange your holders. Do you want two tall ones in the back? Two to three medium on each side? One smaller in front? It really depends on how many brushes you have of each and what size they are. I knew I had a lot of tall shadow and powder brushes, so I needed two or three taller holders.

    To make a tall holder, cut a tube in half, and stack that half on top of a single tube, using hot glue to secure them. The tube just as it is will be perfect for stuff like shorter brushes, scissors, tweezers, and eyelash curlers. The small ones (cut a tube in half or three-quarters) are good for things like sponges or cotton swabs.

2. Place a tube on top of the white cardboard and trace a circle with it. This will become the bottom of each holder. Cut the circle out, then use hot glue to attach to one end of the tube. Allow it to dry for a few minutes. Repeat with each tube.

3. Paint the inside of each tube white. Let dry for at least 20 minutes.

4. Roll printed paper around the outside of each tube; measure and cut to fit, then use hot glue

to secure. Repeat for each tube, and feel free to coordinate the colors and patterns any way you like! You can even add stickers, jewels, or glitter— whatever makes you happy!

5. Now use the hot-glue gun to arrange and attach the tubes to each other. A few dots down the seam of each side will do it. I did two large (1/2 tube) holders in back, three medium (single tube) in front of them, and one small one (1/2 tube) in front of those. Let everything dry overnight before you fill with your brushes and tools. It looks super cute on a vanity or dresser top!

ASK KENZIE

I'm getting braces this week and it's freaking me out! I know I'm going to look so ugly!

When I was little, my teeth were pretty bad. I had gaps between the front ones and a big overbite. But then I went to the ortho and got braces and now I love, love, love my smile! I have to say I was kind of okay with getting them on. It made me feel "teenage" even though I wasn't yet. Plus all the girls on my dance team including my sister got them at practically the same time as me. I think you'll find that a lot of kids you know are dealing with a mouth full of metal while you are—so, like they say in *High School Musical*, you're "all in this together." I won't tell you it's a barrel of laughs or that it didn't hurt whenever they tightened them (ouch!). But I will tell you it's so worth it in the end. Try not to stress, make sure they give you plenty of wax (you'll need it to put on wherever it feels sharp), and drink lots of yummy ice-cold Frappuccinos and milk-shakes while you're getting used to it (good excuse, right?). I know I sound like my mom when I say this, but "we all go through it."

Ugh, I am always breaking out! How can I stop it from happening?

I hate it just as much as you do when a pimple pops up. Make sure to apply an acne product (most contain salicylic acid) the minute you see any redness or swelling; it will help dry up the zit and calm it down. You know, of course, that being a teenager means your skin breaks out a lot more often: My mom says to blame it on hormones, which make more oil. The best way to prevent a breakout is to take really good care of your skin in the first place: Wash it every morning and every night, and take off all your makeup (never go to bed with it on). It's also a good idea to exfoliate once a week with a gentle exfoliating cleanser (I like to use one in the shower, when the steam opens up my pores). The rest of the time, if you're really prone to breakouts, you can try a daily cleanser made for acne-prone skin. Don't borrow your friend's makeup, don't use products that are expired, and never, ever (this is a big one!) pick a pimple. It can cause the zit to get infected and even leave a permanent scar on your skin. I'm always tempted, but Maddie smacks my hand away! Last resort: Go see a dermatologist who can really help you get things under control.

Ew! I hate my freckles! How can I cover them up?

Aw, I think freckles are so cute! A lot of people do, and hopefully one day you will, too. But in the meantime, if you really don't love the "natural" look, you can use a non-cakey full-coverage concealer in a shade that's between the color of your skin and the color of your freckles. If you use one that's too light, it won't do the trick. Blend it in, then apply your foundation and finally a dusting of powder.

RULE 6
EXPAND YOUR HORIZONS

"SEEING THE WORLD OPENS YOUR EYES."

I tend to forget stuff all the time. My mom calls it "teen brain" and complains, "Mackenzie, you would forget your head if it wasn't attached to your neck." I can't help it! I'm just so busy thinking about a million different things at once (my music, ordering takeout, checking my Insta) that things tend to slip through the cracks. But there's one thing I would hate to forget: all the amazing places I've been to all over the world. When we were little, we used to buy a magnet from every city we went to, and our fridge in Pittsburgh was covered in them. And in the olden days (when my mom was a teenager, lol), they used to make scrapbooks. But I think today's kids have lots of cooler options thanks to the world of technology. I found this cool app called VHS Camcorder that lets you piece together a video with a retro time stamp—it looks like I made it in the '80s! I used it to make my vlog of our tour stop in Toronto, and then I shared it with fans.

• •

AWESOME APPS FOR
TRAVEL MEMORIES

There are so many ways you can preserve your vacay moments—that way you'll never forget them, teen brain or not!

» VideoFX lets you customize your video with music, effects, text, etc. It's like you're making a real movie of your trip, complete with score and special effects.

» Shutterfly, Mosaic Photo Books, Groovebook, and Artifact Uprising are great for creating instant photo scrapbooks without any glue! Just upload your photos on the app and they create the book for you.

» 1 Second Everyday strings together the clips you shoot
into a continuous movie. You can literally put together
a whole week's trip in a few seconds.

» The MyMemories app creates a digital scrapbook
that you can share with friends and family—so they
don't feel like they're missing out.

» Framebridge lets you choose your fave photo and
custom-frame it right on your phone. By the time you
get home from your trip, it's already on its way to you
to be hung on your bedroom wall!

• •

I'm lucky—I've seen a lot of the world because of my tours
and TV show: Australia, England, Ireland, Canada, Aruba, Ha-
waii, France, Poland, the Netherlands, Austria, and tons and
tons of cities across the US. I don't want to forget a single moment. I keep a box filled with all the stuff my fans have given
me: notes, photos, bracelets, cards. I used to think of travel as
just "vacation," a time to chill and not think about anything at
home. But now I see it as something more: an opportunity to
better understand what life is like outside your own backyard.
We all assume that everyone does things the way we do, but

I've seen just how different things are, everything from food and fashion to music and customs.

Paris: My whole dance team and I went to the top of the Eiffel Tower and wore the same pink poodle dresses with matching berets! I remember we posed in front of the Louvre museum and the Arc de Triomphe, and the Pont des Arts, a bridge where people leave "love locks" with messages on them. It was always fun traveling with the girls and our moms and meeting all the fans around the world who loved the show so much.

The UK: Johnny and I found this cool mural in the UK that said RUDE KIDS and took videos in front of it! We played Oxford, London, Birmingham, and Sheffield—so I feel like a real Brit now! I can do the accent pretty well, but I have to admit, Johnny does it better—he sounds like Harry Potter. What I love most about the UK is it's a foreign country and the national language is English—so I'm not stressing to figure out how to ask someone on the street, "Where is my hotel?" London to me feels like a cleaner, kinder version of New York or L.A. The city has a lot of energy and a lot of things to do, but everyone is so polite! Plus they have a real queen and princesses there. I used to think they existed only in Disney movies!

Australia: I remember the first time we went with our *Dance Moms* cast, Maddie and I got to cuddle a koala (like a real teddy bear!) and pet a kangaroo. So, so amazing—and I remember I wore this big hat so I'd look like I belonged in the outback. We've been there a lot more times now, and we actually met Jack, Maddie's BF, on our first *Dance Moms* Australian tour, which was crazy: thirteen shows in fourteen days! Maddie and I did our own Aussie tour last year for three weeks, and I vlogged all about it. We started on Hamilton Island, which is in Queensland and has incredible beaches. We managed to get in some swimming and paddleboarding before it poured! Then we hit Melbourne, Adelaide, Brisbane, Perth, the Gold Coast, and Sydney (which, incidentally, has a giant Ferris wheel and a giant Sephora!). Some of the coolest things in Australia are their names for McDonald's (Macca's) and Burger King (Hungry Jack's). I guess they have to give it their own spin? I got to sing and dance before huge crowds and take pics with all our fans. It felt like a whirlwind, but it was wonderful.

A FEW OF MY FAVE THINGS FROM AROUND THE WORLD

Friendliest people: Australia. They're so warm, and they greet you with "G'day!" in their cute accents.

Tastiest cuisine: London. They have such yummy little sandwiches and pastries at high tea. And they're so small you can eat a ton of them.

Weirdest cuisine: Australia. Vegemite is gross. It even sounds gross. What is it, you ask? "A thick, black Australian food spread made from leftover brewers' yeast extract with various vegetable and spice additives." I know—really not appealing! Also, I got a burger in Australia and it didn't taste like a burger, which scares me, but I was afraid to ask what the "meat" was. Plus the Coke cans are really small—like half the size. What's that about?

Best shopping: London again! I went to the Topshop flagship and they had new things that they don't have in the States yet. The store was huge and mind-blowing—like a block long.

Yummiest desserts: Paris. The desserts are so decadent and have fancy names like *éclair*, *petit four*, and *crêpe suzette*. You know if it sounds good it *is* good.

Coolest sights: London. Everything feels so royal and historic there. We saw Big Ben, Buckingham Palace, and the London Bridge. And the red phone booths on the streets! Very Instagrammable.

Country that surprised me the most: Canada. I thought Toronto would look different and "foreign," but honestly, it looks exactly like New York!

Place I'd love to live one day: L.A. full-time. I'm a West Coast girl at heart. If we're talking out of the States, I'd probably pick Canada. The shopping and food are good, and the people are so nice. What else could you ask for in a foreign country?

Place I'd love to go back and visit again: Australia. The beaches are breathtaking and the weather is perfect year-round. It's my happy place.

A DAY IN THE LIFE OF MY TOUR

Eek, where do I begin? I feel like when we're on tour, the hours fly by and it's all such a whirlwind of meeting, greeting, and performing for the best fans all over the globe. Recently I was traveling, and I kept a diary of my day (yeah, it was actually *this* crazy!):

I wake up and hit the ground running! I usually eat yogurt or something quick—there's no time for a fancy, full meal. Often we have interviews to do in the morning and have to be ready. We visit local press outlets and sometimes do an acoustic song to promote the tour. Most of the time, we have an ultimate VIP with fans in the early afternoon and there is pizza, so if I go light on breakfast I save room for it! If it isn't a show day and we're in a hotel, I love ordering room service. It's one of my favorite things to do.

Sometimes I sleep on a bus. I actually don't mind it—it's like a rolling slumber party, with me; Johnny; Lauren (if she's with us); Kylee Renee, who opens for us; plus my two dancers, Rumer Noel and Helene Alam. We aren't in cities very long. We usually do a show and head to the next city immediately after. When we were traveling in Poland one week, our bus actually broke down! We were stuck on the side of the road for a bit and then ultimately had to spend a big part of the day at a gas station. They had to send a Sprinter van to get us so that we could make it to Gdańsk in time for our show. We cut it so close, but we made it.

I miss my family. Not seeing them for weeks at a time is hard. I call my mom every single day and fill her in on where we are, what we saw, what we've been up to. If I'm lucky, I get to squeeze in some sightseeing during a few hours of downtime. When we were in Paris, we got to go to the Eiffel Tower at night and see it all lit up! It was beautiful, and I messaged my mom photos so she could feel like she was there with me.

I usually get ready at the venue. I arrive in comfy clothes and then get ready for the show—hair, makeup, the outfit I'm wearing for that evening. We do a sound check before our meet and greets. We have a band that plays with us but I also have tracks. The guitarist does acoustic songs with me, and some of my dance-based tracks are prerecorded so I'm not panting (singing and dancing full-out is really hard to do!). We don't have background singers, so it's nice to keep the background vocals on the track. Our show is around ninety minutes in total. I sing a selection of my original songs, some covers, and then three songs with Johnny.

I love meeting fans! There are always kids who bring homemade signs. I love seeing them and sometimes I put photos of them on my Snapchat! The venues are always different—I love seeing the different theaters, clubs, and spaces. Usually there are between five hundred and a thousand people. I see people with my face on their shirts, or sometimes they come in clothes from my Justice collection. It's really cool!

I hang out after the show. I like to shower, then just chill out. We might have a dance party on the bus, watch movies together, or play games. Right now we are obsessed with playing Crazy Eights as a group. Even though I should be tired, I usually have a lot of energy after the show. Playing to a live audience and hearing the applause really revs me up. It makes it hard to go to bed early! I try to go to bed by midnight or 1 a.m. If I'm lucky, I can sleep the next day till 10 a.m. and shake off some of the jet lag. It's a real thing! It takes me so long to adjust to a new time zone, and when we travel, I get all messed up and my body can't figure out what time it is. That's another reason I find it hard to go to bed early!

I wouldn't trade this experience for anything. It's so exciting to see the world, to meet fans, to do what I love every day. Sometimes I might complain that I'm tired, but I know how lucky I am. I have to pinch myself from time to time so I actually believe this is my life.

LET ME ENTERTAIN YOU— AT THE AIRPORT

Somehow, my mom always manages to get us to the airport super early, and I'm stuck waiting three hours till we board. That's a lotta time to spend sitting around in the Sky Club twiddling your thumbs! So I've had to come up with some rules for beating airport boredom:

» Hit the magazine racks. Airports always have the latest issues, so I scoop up a bunch of fashion and gossip magazines to get up to speed on the latest news (wait! Justin and Selena are dating again?!) and trends I *need* to buy. Can you say "online shopping"?

» Get a relaxing massage. Many airports have vibrating massage chairs and mini salons where you can get your tired, aching muscles rubbed while you wait.

» Sample some cool cuisine. Have you noticed that there is *every* kind of food you can imagine at the airport, from juices, smoothies, and salads to pizza, sushi, and Chinese? And I haven't even mentioned the desserts: cinnamon buns, hot pretzels, cupcakes. If you're early, you might as well eat!

» Catch up on your fave TV show. When I was in Canada, Lauren shot ahead of me on *The Vampire Diaries*, so now I'm trying to reach the season she's on so she can't spoil it for me. If I have a three-hour wait for a flight, that's three whole episodes of Damon, Stefan, and Elena I can get through. Yes!

» Download some new tunes. There's always free Wi-Fi at the airport, so I use it to load up my phone with a new album or two I've been dying to listen to. Check out the iTunes charts for the latest and greatest—just don't forget your earbuds (because airports are loud).

» Strike up a friendly conversation. This is my mom's specialty! She will always chitchat with someone sitting at our gate, usually a lady carrying a cute dog. Then she pulls out her phone and starts showing pictures of Maliboo. . . .

» Go on a shopping spree. Some airports have entire malls inside them! JFK in New York literally has

B ehind the scenes pics from my "Breathe" shoot!

I'm so lucky that I get to go to so many events!

At the premiere of *Leap!*

Another day, another event!

The three amigos!
I love them so much.

Me and Lauren. We always have a blast when we are together, which is always!

Johnny loves shopping with us . . .

FUN FACT! My nickname for Lauren is Lolo.

BFFs ♥

Had a blast singing in my hometown with Johnny!

In my happy place.

Family selfie time!

There's always time for dessert!

Photo courtesy of author

Sunning with my Maisy.

Photo courtesy of a

I think my T-shirt pretty much sums it up!

Photo courtesy of Glenn Nutley

SOLD OUT!
So incredible!

Our audiences were always the best! This tour was so much fun!

Johnny and I got to experience
so many cool places.

I love performing! I'm clearly having the time of my life!

It's hard not to laugh when Johnny and I perform together.

Taking selfies on my fans' phones!

I truly love what I do.
How lucky am I?!

a Coach store, a Victoria's Secret, and a Juicy Couture right there! Besides clothing, there's perfume, makeup, and every kind of candy you can imagine. I can think of worse ways to kill time.

» Make a vlog. I break out my Canon PowerShot G7 X camera and start making a video that I'll edit later on. I'm never bored if I'm talking on camera and people-watching.

PACK LIKE A PRO

Because I've traveled so much, I've gotten really good at packing all my stuff into one suitcase—it's a talent. I could seriously live an entire week on just the things I squeeze into a single piece of luggage that can be stored under my seat. Of course, there's a science to it:

» Wear any bulky clothes on the plane instead of jamming them in your suitcase. I'm usually in an oversize hoodie or a sweatshirt (a good thing, since airplanes are often chilly). If you're going someplace cold where you need a warm jacket, wear it on the plane as well, or tie it around your waist then stow it up above. A puffer can take up half your packing space!

» Roll anything you can—tees, sweaters, cotton pants, or shorts—and place items tightly next to each other in the luggage. Not only will doing so save space, but it prevents wrinkling.

» Think "travel size." If you don't have mini-size toiletries, buy a few small plastic bottles and fill them with your fave shampoo, conditioner, body wash, etc. Then pack them all into a large Ziploc bag so they won't spill. Don't forget some liquid detergent in a small bottle, too—in case you need to wash stuff out in the sink and re-wear it.

» Pack one pair of "going out" shoes (booties or wedges) and wear a pair of "walking around" shoes (e.g., sneakers) on the plane. Literally, I could live in my black or white Vans all week with every outfit. I also always tuck in a pair of flip-flops for walking around the hotel hallways or hitting the pool.

» Choose pieces that you can mix and match. Limit your options (I know it's hard) to five bottoms (jeans, joggers, a denim skirt/shorts, flowy shorts, leggings); five tops (three tees, one off-the-shoulder shirt, one tank/cami); two jackets (one denim, one dressier bomber in velvet, satin, or vegan leather); one cute dress or romper. Pack a pair of underwear for each day, three or four pairs of socks, two or three bras in neutral colors (nude, white), one strapless bandeau if your outfits need it, and a bathing suit if you plan on swimming.

» Use a large Ziploc bag to pack accessories: some cute bracelets, a belt, a baseball cap, sunglasses, headbands, etc. The rule is it has to fit in the one plastic bag! There's no need to change your earrings or necklace; I just wear mine on the plane. I'm always afraid if I don't they'll get lost or broken.

» I have a large makeup bag that I take on every trip—it has my fave colors and products duplicated from my home makeup kit. If I ever left it at home, I'd be lost! Go through it every so often and toss out products that you've had too long (I once had a mascara in there for like two years—ick!) and replenish. Also, tuck in a good brush and a straightening or curling iron if you use one. Hotels will always have a blow-dryer, so there's no need to pack one.

» Take a small tote for stuff you need during the flight—I carry a backpack that can fit my laptop (with an entire season of my latest binge-worthy show downloaded), some magazines, a book, headphones, snacks. Oh, and slime! I play with slime on the plane! I might also pack a wristlet or small clutch in my tote, which also functions as my wallet for the trip (but looks cute at night).

» It's also a good idea to pack some extra Ziploc bags (for wet and dirty stuff) and a large foldable tote bag—just in case you go shopping and come home with more than you came with. I've also used mine as a beach bag!

A FAB FACE, POST-FLIGHT

Ever wonder how some celebs step off an airplane looking *ah-may-zing* even after an eight-hour flight? I asked my makeup artist Glenn Nutley and he said all it takes is a little TLC for your skin and hair *while* you're in the air.

» Hydrate! A plane takes outside air and circulates it in the cabin through a filtration system that sucks out the humidity. Your skin, throat, and eyes can all feel itchy and parched! Drink water during the flight, even more than you would usually sip.

» Prep before you nap. Cleanse your face with a makeup wipe, remove mascara (you don't want to wake up with raccoon eyes), and moisturize really well.

» Sleep with eye patches and lip balm, so you don't wake up with puffy eyes and cracked lips.

» Brush your hair out and put it in a loose braid or a ponytail so you don't deplane with a bird's nest.

» Ten minutes before you land, it's time to freshen up! Ask for a glass of ice water and wet a facecloth (pack one in your purse). Apply to your eyes for a few minutes to de-puff!

» Use a makeup wipe again, moisturize, apply concealer where needed, slick on a lip balm or stain, swipe on a coat of mascara, and take your hair out of the braid or pony and give it a good brush.

THE KENZIE QUIZ
OH, THE PLACES I SHOULD GO . . .

Not sure where in the world you should travel to in the future? Take this quiz and check your answers on the next page—then get your passport ready.

1. **When you picture your perfect vacay you see yourself:**
    a. *Hiking up a mountain*
    b. *Lying on a pink beach*
    c. *Sightseeing at historical landmarks*

2. **You'd describe yourself as:**
    a. *Sporty*
    b. *Laid-back*
    c. *Curious*

3. **What food sounds yummy to you?**
    a. *A green smoothie*
    b. *A fresh tropical salad*
    c. *An exotic local dish you've never sampled before*

4. **What do you envision on your feet?**
   a. *A pair of skis*
   b. *Nothing—you prefer to go barefoot*
   c. *Comfy walking shoes*

5. **When you need to relax, you:**
   a. *Go for a jog*
   b. *Zone out by the pool*
   c. *Read a historical novel*

If you answered mostly As: A sporty trip is in your future—how about backpacking across the country, skiing the Swiss alps, or zip-lining in Costa Rica? Your ideal vacay is all about action; you like to try new things that challenge your body as well as your mind. Sounds like a blast to me!

If you answered mostly Bs: You're a beach bunny who craves sun, sand, and surf. Why not try Aruba, one of my fave vacation spots (although I did get so sunburnt there I looked like a lobster!), or even a cruise that docks in lots of tropical ports. You enjoy a trip that's big on R & R and not much else. Why not? You deserve it!

If you answered mostly Cs: A European vacation is on your horizon. You'd love roaming through ruins in Rome or Greece, visiting the Louvre in Paris, or taking high tea in London. Anything that's rich in culture is cool in your book (mine, too!).

DON'T UNDERESTIMATE THE AWESOMENESS OF A STAYCATION!

Sometimes my family doesn't go away during a break or holiday; we just hang at home, and I have to admit, it can be more fun than going somewhere exotic. There's a lot to be said for scoping out your hometown for hidden treasures. Case in point: Did you know Pittsburgh has the coolest zoo, a bicycle museum, and a robot hall of fame? I didn't either—not until we were back from L.A., just chilling with our neighbors and googling things to do nearby besides the Dairy Queen and the mall! I love when people come to visit us, because I get to do all sorts of fun and touristy things I would never normally do. I kind of take my hometown for granted (don't we all?). Here's how to have a fun-tastic time right in your own backyard:

» Hit up your hometown newspaper. It will let you know what interesting events are going on, from free yoga workouts and nature hikes to parties and movie screenings.

» Plan your time wisely. Look up hours for museums, stores, parks, etc., you want to visit, and plot out your day. That way you can pack in even more fun!

» Act like a kid—even if you're a teen! I really love checking out stuff I used to like when I was little—like the local children's museum, zoo, playground, toy store, etc. You can act silly and goofy with your friends and no one will tell you to "grow up"!

» On that note, play Dora the Explorer. I used to love watching her on TV when I was little ("Swiper, no swiping!"). Get out a map, a backpack, and a camera and wander around the great outdoors snapping nature pics. It's amazing how many cool critters (birds, bunnies, squirrels), trees, lakes, and flowers you'll spy that make for great Instagrammable pics.

» Organize a scavenger hunt. This is so much fun to do with a large group of friends! Create a crazy list of things to find (a discarded gum wrapper, a penny from 1999, mustache glue, cactus juice, a newspaper that's three days old, etc.). Create a map of places you can search, then send everyone on their way (if it requires driving, an adult will have to chaperone). The first one back to your place with all the items wins!

» Host an at-home game tournament! Break out the board games (Monopoly, Trivial Pursuit, Candy Land, etc.) and invite friends over for the ultimate show-down. Pop popcorn, order in pizza (or make your own chocolaty ones; see the next page), crank up the tunes, and roll those dice!

DIY DESSERT PIZZA

Ingredients:

✳ 1 package refrigerated chocolate chip cookie dough
   (like Pillsbury or Nestlé), at room temperature

✳ Hot fudge sauce

✳ Assorted toppings: whipped cream, sprinkles,
   M&M's, chocolate chips

✳ Nonstick cooking spray

You'll also need:

✳ A pizza pan

✳ Tinfoil

1. Preheat the oven to 350 degrees. Line the pizza
    pan with foil and spray it with cooking spray.

2. Open the cookie dough and roll it with the palms
    of your hands into a circle that fills the pan—this
    will be your pizza crust. Don't make it too thin or
    it will crumble and fall apart when you slice it.
    Keep it about a half-inch thick all around, with
    a little extra thickness at the edges so it looks
    authentically pizza-like.

3. *Bake for 15 minutes or until golden brown. Cool completely.*

4. *Now comes the fun part! Gather your guests round and top that pizza with everything but the kitchen sink! I like to drizzle on hot fudge and do dollops of whipped cream that look like mozzarella cheese! Then we sprinkle on sprinkles and tons of candy—this is a pizza with the works. When you're all done decorating, slice it up and serve with a scoop of ice cream on the side. Can you say "yum"?*

KENZIE'S CRAFT CORNER

OLD-SCHOOL MEMORY JAR

Any adventure is worth revisiting. This is a way to keep your memories tidy and on display.

WHAT YOU'LL NEED:

* *Jars of assorted sizes and colors*
* *Souvenirs from your trip that will fit inside (ticket stubs, sand, seashells, postcards, pine cones, foreign coins—you get the idea! Anything that reminds you of your adventure)*
* *A Sharpie*
* *Pretty ribbon*

1. Remove any labels from the jar (you might need to soak them for a while).
2. Fill the jar with anything you've found or bought on your trip. You can use a little hot glue to make these items "stand up" on the bottom of the jar, but I like mine scattered and loose.
3. Seal the jar with the lid.
4. Using your Sharpie, label the lid with the place and time where you got the jar's contents, like PARIS, SEPT. 2017. Tie a ribbon around the neck of the jar to make it look pretty. I choose colors that remind me of my travels: for example, red, white, and blue for the colors of the British flag; coral for the sun in Aruba. You can display your jars on a shelf or dresser top. I like to look at mine every now and then to remind me of all the great times I've had.

ASK KENZIE

I'm going to sleepaway camp for the first time this summer—and I'm really nervous. What if I don't like being away from my parents and my little brother and miss them like crazy?

There were a bunch of times I had to be away from my mom or Greg or Maddie or even Maliboo, and I did miss them a lot. But those feelings are normal: Missing people just means you love them. I used to fight with my sister all the time and wish she would just go away and stop bugging me—and then she went out on tour with Sia. At first I was psyched: I had our home all to myself. Then something hit me: I really, really missed having her around. I was sad, and I couldn't wait to Skype or call her. You might feel the same when you're away, especially at first, when you're adjusting to a new place and new people. Just recently, I had to go on tour, and my mom and Maddie stayed back in L.A. because Maddie was working on a movie—which meant I was far, far away from them. I try not to think about it like that; I tell myself I'll have so many cool things to share with my family when I get home. I try hard to just be in the present and enjoy the moment. Don't let your fears hold you back from having what could be an amazing adventure this summer. Most people who go to camp say it's the best time ever—and they make tons of new friends who become like family. Give yourself a little pep talk—"I can do this, it's gonna be great"—and know that if you *weren't* homesick, that would be weird.

My entire Girl Scout troop is going on a whitewater rafting trip and my parents won't let me go! They think it could be "dangerous."

What's freaking them out—are they afraid you're too young to go? That you're not a strong swimmer? That the ride might be fast and bumpy and you could fall out? Sit them down and calmly tell them how much you want to go and why. Is this an experience you've always dreamed about? Is it a great opportunity for you to get to know the other girls better? Will you be the only kid *not* going? Can you talk to your troop leader and get her to assure your parents that you will be safe and sound and wear a life vest? Parents sometimes set rules that can be frustrating—been there, done that. My mom has vetoed so many things I want to do. I remember after our "Day & Night" video shoot, Johnny and Lauren wanted to go ice-skating. I asked my mom and she was like, "No way! You'll fall! You'll break a leg! You'll kill yourself!" Such an overreaction! Or a couple of times, my friends wanted to go indoor skydiving and my mom freaked and said, "Not before a big event!" It's not like I'm going to float away and miss the event! But parents always have a really good reason for their fears and concerns. You may not agree with them, but they just love you and worry about you. Not that I'm saying my mom is always right, but I understand that it's coming from her heart.

GREG'S GUIDE TO GETTING YOUR PARENTS TO GIVE IN

So my stepdad is a very fair guy—he will always hear us out, listen to our reasons, and never make a ruling for my sister or me before carefully considering. I asked his advice on how to convince a mom or dad to see things your way—and this is what he had to say:

» "Stay cool. No throwing a tantrum, screaming, yelling, pitching a fit. I know you don't agree with me, but I will not hear you if you shout. If you want me to regard you as a mature young adult, then you must act like one. Talk things through with me calmly and quietly and don't resort to slamming your bedroom door."

» "Make a good case. Explain why it's so important for you to do this. What do you hope to get out of it? The fact that your BFF is doing it is not reason enough. If your friend jumped off a bridge would you do it, too? (Don't answer that!) I'd also be very impressed (and maybe reconsider) if you put together a detailed plan/

proposal and listed how you will be responsible. Address each of my concerns with a sensible solution, like 'I will always make sure to stick with the troop leader and double-check my life preserver is fastened correctly.'"

» "Show me you can be responsible. Convince me! I need to see it in other aspects of your life, e.g., good grades, sticking to curfews, cleaning up your room and pitching in whenever I or your mom ask. If I tell you to text me when you get to a friend's house and you forget, sorry, but that's strike one."

» "Never pit one parent against the other. Don't get your mom on your side; that's an automatic no for me. Don't gang up on this guy!"

» "Acknowledge there are consequences. If I *do* give in, know that you have to keep all your promises. You can't lie to me, and you have to prove that my trust was justified. If not, it ain't happening again!"

» "Finally, say thank you! Anything your mom or dad does probably comes from a place of love and care.

Even if you don't get your way right away, it's nice for a parent to hear 'I understand where you're coming from.' And if I do give in, then say the magic word: 'Thanks!'"

Help! I have to go on a school trip and all we can take is a backpack for five days. Are they kidding me? I usually take two huge duffel bags and a carry-on for a weeklong vacation!

Okay, you need to see my packing tips on page 139 because that sounds like way too much luggage! In terms of this trip, pare down—literally. You don't need several pairs of shoes, jeans, underwear, etc. You can re-wear things and wash them—every day doesn't require a new outfit. Give yourself a challenge: How many outfits can you mix and match from a few tops and bottoms? Leave the extra accessories at home and keep the makeup and toiletries to a small cosmetics bag. I promise, you'll feel so much lighter traveling this way, and choosing an outfit every day will be a breeze—you won't have to weed through a closet full of options. You can keep it simple and still be stylish!

RULE 7
YOU CAN MAKE A PARTY ANYWHERE

"JUST ADD FRIENDS AND FUN . . . AND MIX!"

G o ahead, call me a party animal: I've thrown a bunch of amazing parties. Some have had themes, like "Fashion Runway" or "Teen Beach Movie." Others have had a specific color scheme. I had two thirteenth-b-day parties, one in L.A. and one in Pittsburgh. For the L.A. one, I invited thirty people, and they brought their friends, and they brought their friends, and before I knew it there was a huge crowd! We held it at a dance studio with disco lights and a photo booth, and it was so much fun. At home, I had a more mellow joint party with my friend Kylie. Our family friend Nina Linhart did all the organizing and threw me one of the best parties of my life. It was in June at the Double-Tree in Monroeville, Pennsylvania. We rented a ballroom, and Nina designed my theme around a cool cake I found on Pinterest: It was two-tiered and white with black polka dots, a hot-pink bow made of fondant, and rhinestone trim. But what caught my eye was the fondant face on the bottom tier: It had hot-pink lips and two eyes with long lashes winking! I loved how girly and sassy it was, and also the colors of the cake: white, pink, black, and silver. Nina didn't tell me all the details of what she was planning with my mom; she wanted me to be surprised. We sent out invitations online to thirty of our dance studio friends and I counted down the days till the event.

Finally, it was the morning of June 4. I spent a good part of the afternoon getting ready. I wore a cute floral dress with a lace bralette underneath and sneakers. They didn't really go (heels would have been a more stylish choice), but I wanted to be able to dance.

It was hard to miss the party space: There was a giant poster of me with my friends and a pink carpet (instead of a red carpet) leading into the ballroom. Nina also hung huge balloons—a hot-pink *K* and a silver *1* and *3*. Inside, there was exactly the cake I had wanted, displayed on a rhinestone cake stand on a black tablecloth. There were pink plates and nap-kins, and Nina had also sprinkled rhinestones around on ta-bletops for some added bling. She set up a candy bar with every pink, white, and silver M&M, jellybean, and gummy she could get her hands on and displayed them in super-fun bowls and vases. And of course, we had a DJ and a photo booth to cap-ture images of this amazing night. The food was served buffet style and included all of my faves: chicken fingers, mac and cheese, french fries. Nina even put out bowls of Doritos on all the tables—since it wouldn't be a Kenzie celebration without my chips!

When I cut the cake, the inside layers alternated between chocolate and vanilla with buttercream icing. As I looked around the room, I saw the faces of all my friends and fam-ily smiling at me, and I realized (here comes the cheesy part!) the best gift I received was getting to be surrounded by people who love me.

PLANNING THE PERF PARTY

Whether you're planning a big bash or a small sleepover, it helps to start with the basics. I usually take out a notebook and start jotting stuff down. . . .

Who: Who will the guests be and how many of them will you invite? Will you send out paper invites or e-vites?

What: What's the occasion? Is there something special you're celebrating?

Where: Where will the party take place? In a ballroom, a backyard, the basement of your house?

When: What is a good date and time to throw the party? Are you thinking a morning brunch, afternoon pool party, or dinner and dancing?

How: How will you organize your party, prepare the food, hire the DJ, send out the invites, etc.? Is your parent or a sibling or friend going to pitch in? What's the budget for the event: How much money can you reasonably spend on it?

Once you know the logistics, it's time to get creative (my favorite part) and brainstorm all the details. A party needs a great theme—it's the glue that holds everything together. Your theme can be anything, from a favorite movie or celeb to an exotic locale. It can be timed to a holiday (Valentine's, Halloween, Christmas) or a period in time (the '50s, '60s, '70s, '80s . . .). Here are a few of my fave themes I've tried out and some ideas for executing them. Remember, what makes a party great is three simple things: the people, the music, and the food.

THEME: FASHION RUNWAY

Guests will . . . get their glam on and walk a "runway" after creating their ideal outfit from boxes of accessories (hats, bags, boas, tiaras, gloves, sunglasses) or racks of clothes you provide. They can style themselves or each other on teams. Pump up the music and tell everyone to strut like a supermodel!

Décor: Roll out a red carpet (you can find them at a party store), throw up some velvet curtains, or draw a giant high-heeled shoe on a sheet of poster board, cut it out, and cover with glitter for a dazzling backdrop. You can also have guests cut up fashion magazines and create mood boards, in case they need a little inspiration to channel on the runway! I would make a supermodel collage starring Gigi Hadid and Kendall and Kylie Jenner—my fashion role models.

Party Playlist: "Vogue" by Madonna; "Fashion" by Lady Gaga; "Roll 'Em Up" by Alli Simpson with Jack & Jack; "She's Got the Look" by Roxette; "I'm Too Sexy" by Right Said Fred.

FUN FOOD: "SHOEBIZ" CUPCAKES

I've seen so many of these high-heel cupcakes on Pinterest and always wanted to try them! A party is a great excuse, don't you think? This recipe is super simple; you can make the cupcakes from scratch or a mix or even buy some unfrosted ones at a bakery. If you're having a home party, your guests can decorate and assemble them as a fun activity.

Ingredients:

* 2 containers vanilla frosting
* Liquid food coloring
* 12 cupcakes, unfrosted
* 1 bag Milano cookies
* Colored sugar
* Candy pearls, sprinkles, or other decorations
* 1 box Pirouette cookies
* White chocolate candy melts

You'll also need:

* Small bowls and spoons for mixing

* A microwavable bowl
* Pastry bags and assorted tips

1. Put the frosting in several small bowls and add a few drops of coloring to each bowl, stirring until you achieve your perfect shade.

2. Fit a pastry bag with a tip and scoop in one of your colored frostings—then get piping! Cover the top of each cupcake with a different hue.

3. Decorate with pearls, sprinkles, sugar—anything you want, to make your shoe look haute couture!

4. Use a knife to carefully make a small hole just above the cupcake liner on one side. The sole of your shoe—aka the Milano cookie—will fit in that hole.

5. Take a Milano cookie and frost a thin line around the border. Dip the cookie into the colored sugar, which will stick wherever there is frosting. Place an edge of the Milano in the hole you've made, using some extra frosting to secure it.

6. Take a Pirouette cookie and cut it in half on an angle to fit under the sole of the shoe. This is your heel.

7. Melt 6 candy melts in a microwavable bowl for 30 seconds. Remove from oven, then stir and repeat for two or three more 30-second intervals, until the candy is melted.

8. Dip the angled end of the Pirouette cookie into the candy melts. "Glue" it to the Milano, holding it in place till it dries and hardens.

9. Place your fab footwear on a platter and serve.

THEME: BEAUTY BASH

Guests will . . . get gorge and indulge in mani-pedis, facials, even glitter tattoos. At a large party, you can set up stations for each treatment. If you're having a small at-home party, provide your guests with comfy robes, just like at a spa, and play a game of "blind makeover." Blindfold yourself and do a friend's face without being able to see where you're applying it! I've done this with Maddie and the results are pretty hilarious.

Décor: Tons of makeup palettes, brushes, polishes, and primping tools—practical and pretty! Place makeup mirrors on tables and make sure the lighting is good.

Party Playlist: "Glamorous" by Fergie featuring Ludacris; "Lips Are Movin'" by Meghan Trainor; "What Makes You Beautiful" by One Direction.

FUN FOOD:
NAIL POLISH NIBBLES

These treats look like bottles of polish—perfect for a beauty-themed get-together.

Ingredients:

* Colored sugar crystals
* A container of vanilla frosting
* Liquid food coloring
* A bag of marshmallows
* Tootsie Roll Midgees

You'll also need:

* 4 or 5 small microwave-safe bowls
* 4 or 5 shallow dishes

1. Pour the different-colored sugar crystals into the shallow dishes.
2. Now scoop the frosting into the microwavable bowls (about 2–3 T in each) and heat for 30 seconds.

3. Add 4–6 drops of food coloring to each bowl of melted frosting and stir till you create your perfect color.

4. Dip a marshmallow into the frosting—you'll want to do this fairly quickly, because once the frosting cools, it gets too hard to coat the marshmallow. If you need to, pop the bowl back into the microwave for a few seconds to heat the frosting up again.

5. After you've coated the marshmallow in warm frosting, roll it in a coordinating color of sugar crystals to give it a "shimmery" look. This will be your polish bottle.

6. Once it's cool, use a little pit of frosting to attach a Tootsie Roll to the top of each marshmallow. This will be the "cap" of your bottle. How cute is that?

THEME: TEEN BEACH MOVIE

Guests will . . . don leis and sip tropical-inspired fruit drinks while rocking out to surfer tunes. This is a great theme for a pool party—you can host a "gnarly" bash right in your back-yard!

Décor: Cardboard or inflatable palm trees, beach balls, grass skirts, table linens in neon, tropical colors.

Party Playlist: Soundtrack from *Teen Beach Movie*; anything by the Beach Boys.

FAB FOOD: PINEAPPLE CHICKEN ON A STICK

Serves 6–8

These tropical-inspired kabobs are both sweet and sour and fun to assemble.

Ingredients:

* 4 chicken tenders, cooked (grilled or baked, plain or breaded) and cut into bite-size pieces
* ½ green bell pepper, cut into bite-size pieces
* 2 c. fresh pineapple chunks
* Teriyaki or Hawaiian BBQ sauce

You'll also need:

* Wooden skewers

1. Assemble each stick with alternating chicken, peppers, and pineapple.
2. Serve on a platter with a small bowl of sauce on the side. Yup, it's that easy!

FINGER FOOD FOR ALL OCCASIONS

If I'm throwing a party, I always want apps that people can just grab while they gab. The idea is to offer lots of little snacks and sips that people can dig into without getting distracted from all the fun.

SALSA IN A BLENDER

The fact that you toss everything in and hit BLEND makes this recipe so easy.

Ingredients:

* 1 28-oz. can whole, peeled tomatoes
* 1 small onion, coarsely chopped
* 3 cloves garlic, coarsely chopped
* 1 ½ tsp. ground cumin
* 1 ½ tsp. salt
* ½ tsp. granulated sugar
* 1 c. cilantro leaves with stems removed
* 3 T lime juice
* Pinch of red pepper flakes (to give it some kick!)
* Bag of corn chips, for dipping

1. Throw all the ingredients into a blender and pulse on high for about a minute. It's really personal—I like my salsa easy to scoop up, so I leave it on the chunky side. Blend longer if you like it smooth, and you can always add more red pepper flakes or even a chopped jalapeño pepper to the ingredients if you like it extra spicy.
2. Pour the salsa into a bowl and serve with chips.

MINI DEEP-DISH PIZZAS

These are not only cute but taste great, too.

Ingredients:

* 1 tube crescent roll dough (I used Pillsbury)
* 1 package shredded mozzarella cheese
* 1 jar pizza sauce
* 4 pepperoni snack sticks, cut into slices
* Nonstick cooking spray

You'll also need:

* A muffin pan
* Wax paper
* A small plastic cup

1. Preheat the oven to 375 degrees.
2. Open the dough and lay it on the wax paper on a table or on top of a cookie sheet (you want a hard surface).
3. Use the rim of the small plastic cup to punch out 12 small circles.
4. Spray the muffin pan with cooking spray and put a dough circle into each hole.

5. Sprinkle mozzarella cheese on top of the dough (this keeps it from getting soggy), then spoon some sauce on top.

6. Add another sprinkling of cheese, then top with your mini pepperoni slices.

7. Bake for 15 minutes, until the cheese starts to bubble and the crust turns golden brown. Take them out of the oven and allow them to sit for about five minutes before using a fork to gently pop them out.

BERRY DELICIOUS LEMONADE

I feel like every party needs some lemonade—this one has a sweet twist.

Ingredients:

* 1 pint raspberries
* 1 ½ c. strawberries, stems removed and cut in half
* 2 c. freshly squeezed lemon juice
* ½ c. grated lemon peel
* 1 c. sugar
* 6–8 cups cold water

You'll also need:

* A potato masher
* A fine mesh strainer
* 2 large bowls
* A wooden spoon
* A glass pitcher for serving

1. In one of the large bowls, place the raspberries, strawberries, lemon juice, lemon peel, and sugar.

2. Now comes my fave part: Use the potato masher to smush all the fruit together and dissolve the sugar. You can also use a food processor or blender, but I think this is much more fun!

3. Pour the mixture into the strainer holding it over a large bowl and using a wooden spoon to push it against the mesh and get out as much juice as you can. You should have about 2 cups of red liquid, which you will pour into the pitcher.

4. Now add the water and garnish it with some lemon slices and whole strawberries.

5. Chill in the fridge and serve, or pour into glasses containing ice.

KENZIE'S CRAFT CORNER

CUPCAKE LINER STREAMERS

You just need some leftover liners (about 3 dozen) to make any room look prettier.

WHAT YOU'LL NEED:

* Paper cupcake liners in different colors and designs
* A needle and thread

1. Thread your needle, making a large knot at one end so the liners won't slip off. The thread should be long, about 4–5 feet, so you can string it across a wall. You may want someone to hold one end while you work on stringing.

2. Pierce your needle through the first liner; the bottom of the liner should be facing the knot, and the open end of the liner should be facing you.

3. Now add the second liner, but in the opposite way, with the open side facing the knot. Pull the second liner down the string until the two openings lightly touch.

4. Add the next liner, pushing the needle through with the bottom side facing the knot. You want to keep repeating this pattern, always making sure that the open liners face each other. Change colors and designs as often as you like—you can even make a rainbow effect.

5. When you reach the end, tie another thick knot. You can use the thread to tie the ends to a curtain rod, or tape them above a doorway.

ASK KENZIE

I'm having a bunch of girls over for a slumber party and I don't know what to do with them. Any suggestions?

Um, yeah! Any slumber party I'm throwing includes some slime time! Here are three of my faves. (NOTE: These slimes are *not* edible.)

RAINBOW SLIME

WHAT YOU'LL NEED:

* ½ c. white or clear Elmer's School Glue (if you use white, your colors will be more pastel)
* ½ c. water
* ½ tsp. baking soda
* Food coloring
* 1 T saline (contact lens) solution
* 5 large bowls (one for each color) and spoons

1. Pour the glue and water into a large bowl and stir.
2. Now sprinkle in the baking soda and stir again. Add a few drops (about 4–6) of food coloring into the bowl. Mix until the color is bright (add more food coloring if you need to).
3. Finally, add the saline solution and stir, then knead with your hands until the mixture is gooey and slime-like.
4. Do this for each color you want to make; you can even sprinkle in some glitter to make it shimmery.

For a rainbow effect, I scoop out a little of each color and twist in the palms of my hands, creating rainbow stripes. So pretty and so much fun to play with!

FLUFFY SLIME

WHAT YOU'LL NEED:

* ½ c. white Elmer's School Glue
* 3 c. foam shaving cream
* Liquid food coloring of your choice
* ¼ tsp. baking soda
* 1 T saline solution
* A large bowl
* A spoon

1. Put the glue in a bowl.
2. Add a few drops (4–6) of food coloring and mix. If you want the color darker, add some more drops, one at a time.
3. Add the shaving cream and the baking soda to the bowl and stir.

4. Now add the saline solution and mix.

5. Use your hands now to knead the mixture till it gets slime-like—that's the best part!

GLOW-IN-THE-DARK ALIEN SLIME

WHAT YOU'LL NEED:

* 1 c. white Elmer's School Glue
* ½ c. water
* Neon green glow-in-the-dark paint
* 1 T saline solution
* ½ tsp. baking soda
* A large bowl
* A spoon

1. Pour the glue and water into a large bowl and stir.

2. Now add a few drops of the paint, stirring and adding more until you achieve the color you like.

3. Add the baking soda and the saline solution.

4. Knead with your hands until the slime forms.

5. Glow-in-the-dark slime needs to be charged up to work. Hold it close to a light bulb for a few minutes, then turn off the lights and watch it glow. Out of this world!

RULE 8
IT'S A GIRL THING

irls can be so good at drama—and I don't mean the class you take in school where you recite Shakespeare. I mean the mean girl behavior that involves spreading rumors, backstabbing, icing people out, and generally creating tons of tension when there wasn't any two seconds ago. Drama almost always involves jealousy and competitiveness. No one starts it without a reason, and that reason is usually, "I wish I had what she has." I didn't realize that when I was younger, but now I do, and my absolute rule on the subject is this: Leave me out of it. I'm a drama-free zone! But there are girls who think they can suck me in. Perfect example: I'm checking my Snapchat and I see several of my friends on their stories laughing and having a great time at a party. Where, you ask, am I in all of this? Left out. Excluded. All my friends from back home are there, but not me. Ouch. Then I remind myself that they're posting this *knowing* I will see it. It's a really subtle way of telling me, "You don't belong anymore." Here comes the drama!

I immediately call one of them and ask her what's going on. "Nothing," she tells me. "Everything's fine. We're still friends." But friends don't leave friends out, and they certainly don't gossip about them behind their backs. The same group also complained that I was acting "too serious" about my career and that I wasn't fun anymore. Well, how can I be fun if you don't invite me? So recently, I decided it was time to do a little "editing" when it came to my friend list—and some names got crossed off. It might be hard, but you have to truly weed out your friends from your frenemies. And sometimes it's not that easy to tell the two apart.

THE KENZIE QUIZ
IS SHE A FRIEND OR A FRENEMY?

Consider the gal pals in your life and how they'd handle the following.

1. **You just won first place in a dance competition. Your friend:**
    a. *Jumps up and down and hugs you*
    b. *Smiles and says, "Congrats," then adds, "But you know the competition wasn't all that tough, right?"*
    c. *Whispers to another teammate, "OMG, are those judges blind?"*

2. **You're having a horrible day: You failed your math test. You confide in your friend and she:**
    a. *Listens patiently and lets you vent*
    b. *Pats you on the back and says, "Aw, that's too bad. I got 100."*
    c. *Makes sure everyone at the lunch table knows your score*

3. **Your teacher says you have to choose teams for a science fair project. Your friend:**

a. *Makes sure you and she work in the same group*

b. *Pairs up with the popular clique and tells you, "Sorry! They asked me!"*

c. *Whispers to a few classmates that she had to help you on your last lab*

4. **You wear a new jacket to school. Your friend:**

a. *Oohs and ahs and says you look amazing in it*

b. *Asks if she can borrow it, "because it would look even cuter on me!"*

c. *Waits till she has an audience in study hall, then asks, "What are you wearing?"*

5. **You're totally crushing on a guy in chem class. You tell your friend and she:**

a. *Offers to help you brainstorm ways to get his attention*

b. *Mentions that he was actually scoping her out yesterday—"what a coinky-dink!"*

c. *Tells a friend who tells a friend who tells his friend that you like him—without your permission*

If you answered mostly As: Your friend is a keeper, true-blue, and a BFF to you. She knows what to say and how to listen, and always has your back. She understands what being a good friend is all about: caring, sharing, and appreciating you for who you are.

If you answered mostly Bs: Your friend appears to be a bestie, but be warned—she can be jealous, competitive, and petty. She can't be happy for your triumphs, because she's insecure herself. This is someone who will always try to one-up you—she has definite frenemy potential.

If you answered mostly Cs: Your so-called friend isn't acting like one. She's talking about you behind your back and stirring up trouble. Don't take the bait and don't hesitate: Move on! With friends like her, who needs enemies?

GROWING UP AND APART

When I was little, friendships were so much easier. I had no clue what true friends or fake friends were; I just played with everyone and shared my snacks. It would be great if things could stay that way, but as we get into our tween and teen years, things get, well, complicated. There's more pressure socially to fit in, to make alliances, to belong to a group (the jocks, the popular kids, the brainiacs, etc.). People you thought were "your people" are suddenly not anymore, and that can make you sad and frustrated—especially when it comes out of nowhere. Try to understand that friendships can change—some get weaker, some get stronger, some fade all together. You know how it goes: The girl who was your bestie in elementary school suddenly isn't in your universe anymore. Outta sight, outta mind. In fact, you can't remember the last time you two texted. What happened? Where did she go? Where did "*we*" go?

It used to make me upset, but now I accept that growing up sometimes means growing apart. I look for people I can connect with at *this* stage of my life—girls (and boys, too) who share the same interests and dreams, and who truly "get me." You have to find your "team" and weed out the fakes, phonies, and control freaks who pretend they're on your side while trying to use or manipulate you—and there's a lot of that going on. I have plenty of close friends, but not as many friends in general, like I used to. I've made sure the people around me are only those people I would trust with my life. Yeah, maybe that sounds overly dramatic, but I mean it. I feel like my inner circle is my safety net, and that includes Maddie, my mom, and Greg, too. We would do anything for each other.

A FEW FACTS ABOUT REAL FRIENDS

THIS IS THE STUFF THAT BFFS ARE MADE OF

» Friends don't lie to each other. They will tell you, honestly, if your pants clash with your shirt, or if your hair is frizzy, but in a kind, considerate way—as opposed to broadcasting it across the cafeteria.

» Friends don't judge. They understand that you're entitled to your opinions and choices, and they never hold them against you, even if they don't agree.

» Friends bring out the best in you. They encourage you to dream big, have faith in yourself, and see your potential. They are your biggest fans.

» Friends listen. They never interrupt or lecture; they lend a shoulder to cry on when you need one. They know the value of a hug.

» Friends stick around—even when the going gets tough. They won't desert you if you're in trouble or if things get tricky and complicated. They're loyal with a capital *L*!

» Friends forgive you when you freak out, when you forget their birthday, when you say something that hurts. They may be mad for a little while, but they understand that we're all human and make mistakes.

» Friends keep your secrets. They will never rat you out or share your top-secret info with others. Their lips are sealed!

» Friends remind you how great you are! They always give you a standing ovation and tell you you're special—especially when you're doubting yourself and need to hear it the most.

KENZIE'S CRAFT CORNER

GIVE YOUR BFF A "HAPPY JAR"

I love the idea of making my friend a jar filled with positivity—little words of encouragement she can pull out whenever she needs some. It's like opening a fortune cookie, only better, since each note is personalized just for her.

WHAT YOU'LL NEED:

* A large plastic canister (about 2 quarts)
* Several sheets of colored paper, cut into small, fortune cookie-size strips
* Sharpies

1. Start by finding a bunch of quotes, poems,

affirmations, knock-knock jokes, even inside jokes
your friend would love. If I were doing a jar for
Lauren, some of my happy notes might read:

» You're the best friend—you like me even with
Dorito breath!

» Knock-knock. Who's there? Etch. Etch who?
Bless you!

» What did the buffalo say when his kid left for
college? Bison!

» When in doubt . . . dance it out!

» Why don't you see giraffes in elementary
school? Because they're all in high school!

» "Beauty happens the moment you decide to
be yourself." —Kylie Jenner

2. *Fill the jar up, then label it with something cute,*
   like a poem:

   To Lauren, from Mackenzie: Enjoy this jar of
   happy!
   Whenever you're feeling blue,
   Pull out a note or two.
   From one BFF to another,
   Make sure to keep these from your brother!

ASK KENZIE

I overheard my friend talking about me behind my back! She was in the girls' bathroom and didn't know I was in there, too. She was making fun of me to two of the popular girls in school. I don't know what to do—should I confront her or pretend I don't know?

I had something like this happen to me last year. A girl I thought was my friend started talking about me behind my back. We danced together, and she was always chummy and nice when I was around. But then she would tell everyone lies about me. I'm sorry, but friends don't act like that—ever. If you really think the friendship is worth saving, then yes, talk to her and tell her how hurt you were. But my mom always says, "A leopard doesn't change its spots." I'm not sure she'll quit trying to impress the popular clique at your expense, and if that's the case, you're better off without her.

My BFF went away on a teen tour and came back with a whole bunch of new friends. It's like I never existed! She never has time for me anymore because she's always with them.

Like I said, friends can drift apart, especially over the summer, when people go off and do new things with new people. They bond, and that leaves you out in the cold. Tell your BFF you miss spending time with her. Maybe she has no idea she's ignoring you or hurting your feelings? Try to reconnect, but if it doesn't work, don't sit around feeling sad. Hang out with some new friends and give those relationships a chance to grow—then you won't feel so bad that you've grown apart.

My BFF is a boy—is that so weird?

Actually, I'm friends with more guys than girls. It's a good thing—they can offer you a totally different perspective on stuff (see the next chapter) that you would never get from a gal pal. Most boys are very honest, and most of the time, they don't overdramatize. I don't think it matters if your BFF is male or female, only that he or she is loyal and you have fun hanging out together. Which brings us to my next rule and chapter...

RULE 9
IT'S A GUY THING

At home in Pittsburgh I have a really good friend, Dyson, and (obviously) he's a guy. He's one of my best friends and someone who's always been there for me. I can tell him anything and the same goes for him with me. Then there's Johnny Orlando, who's like a brother—an annoying, practical-joking, burping brother. Then Jack, Maddie's BF, who never gets mad if I'm third-wheeling. I love hanging with the guys.

In first grade, I had a new boyfriend every day, so many it was hard to keep track. I have always had boys on the brain: When we were little, Maddie and I used to fight over who was going to marry Justin Bieber (for the record, I am). When I turned eleven or twelve, I started crushing and getting boy-crazy. My friends all know the signs now: My cheeks get red and I giggle a lot. Being around a cute guy makes me totally tongue-tied, so chances are if I ever bump into Cole Sprouse or Ian Somerhalder I won't be able to say a word! Of course, I would never ask a guy out myself—nuh-uh, no way. I would either ask one of my girlfriends or my sister to do it, or maybe get one of his friends to whisper in his ear. They would put me in his mind, like, "Kenzie's really cute. You should talk to her." It usually works—something about the boy code. It's an unwritten law: If another guy thinks a girl is cute, then it's okay for you to think she's cute and make a move. Oh, brother!

Speaking of brothers, I have two half brothers I love hanging out with: Ryan, who's twenty-five, and Tyler, who's twenty-one. I've gathered a lot of highly classified info on the boy brain from them as well as from my friends who are guys. There's a lot of stuff they don't want you to know (probably because it makes them look less cool). But I'll let you in on a few secrets....

» **Boys feel the same peer pressure girls do:** to be cool, to fit in, to be accepted.

» **Boys go through a really awkward phase.** Lots of stuff starts changing physically, and it's weird and tough to deal with. Lucky for us, our voices don't change!

» **Boys can be insecure.** Sure, they might act tough, but behind the tough-guy façade is a dude who doubts himself big-time!

» **Boys are afraid of being rejected.** It holds them back sometimes from asking you out. What if you say no? How embarrassing would that be? Be kind if they ask; they're sort of fragile.

» **Boys have one-track minds.** Seriously, if they want pizza, all they're thinking about is pizza. Same goes for pretty much anything else they're obsessing over.

» **Boys aren't thinking about marriage.** Not at the moment! So while we're trying on last names (Mrs. Mackenzie Sprouse), they're happy to just hang out.

» **Boys care about their appearance.** Many spend way too much time and money on hair gel and freak if they get a pimple.

» **Boys worry** about their grades, pleasing their parents, global warming—you name it. They're big bundles of nerves, just like us! I've even known a few who bit their nails!

» **Boys need approval.** Pay them a compliment and they light up. A kind word goes a long way.

» **Boys don't understand girls.** They haven't quite figured us out yet, but they'll keep trying!

THE KENZIE QUIZ
DOES YOUR CRUSH LIKE YOU BACK?

Not sure where you stand? His actions speak louder than words!

1. **He texts you:**
    a. *24/7*
    b. *To ask for help on his math homework*
    c. *Never*

2. **If you couldn't find a seat in the lunchroom he would:**
    a. *Scoot over and make room for you next to him*
    b. *Point out a space way over in the corner*
    c. *Let you fend for yourself*

3. **Whenever he's with his friends and you walk by he:**
    a. *Ditches them to go with you*
    b. *Looks up and gives you a quick wave*
    c. *Ignores you—he's too busy with his bros*

4. **When you're together, your crush talks mostly about:**
    a. *How awesome you are*
    b. *The weather*
    c. *Himself*

5. **If you asked him to hang out he would:**

    a.   *Be excited and enthusiastic*

    b.   *Ask, "Why?"*

    c.   *Say he's too busy*

If you answered mostly As: Seriously? You need more proof than this that he's into you? Everything he does and says declares he's equally infatuated. If you're too chicken to make a move, then have a friend tell him you feel the same. You guys are meant to be together!

If you answered mostly Bs: Okay, there's hope: He's kind of on the fence about his feelings. He's polite and cordial— now you need to push him toward "interested." Do something nice (pay him a compliment, bake him cookies, offer him help in class) that shows what a great GF you'd be.

If you answered mostly Cs: Sorry to break it to you, but he's not showing any signs. He seems a little self-absorbed— are you sure you wanna go there? If so, then try flirting or simply strike up a convo in class: He needs to know you're alive before he can have feelings for you.

20 QUESTIONS FOR JOHNNY ORLANDO (IN WHICH I TORTURE MY TOUR PARTNER, LOL)

Mackenzie: Okay, we're starting.

Johnny: We're starting? Like now? Okay, fire away.

M: Question one. Do you remember how and when we first met?

J: Yeah, I do. It was at a studio somewhere in North Hollywood. It was called the Jungle Room. I don't even know why you were there. Maybe you were recording your first album? My producer set up the meeting and it was really awkward. I remember that. I had no idea what to say.

M: I think you said, "Hey."

J: Sounds like me. Short, sweet, to the point.

M: So what was your first impression of me? That's question two.

J: Hmmm. It was kind of awkward, because all my sisters used to watch you on your show. So it was kind of weird for me to see you in person. I remember my sister Maddie was like, "Oh my God, that's so cool. You met Mackenzie!"

M: Really?

J: Yeah. Now, obviously, you're like her little sister, so she doesn't really care.

M: Thanks.

J: But yeah, I thought you were nice. I just knew that you felt super awkward, because you had no idea what to say to us, and I felt the same way.

M: On to number three. Be honest, aren't I an awesome person to tour with day and night—see how I got that pun in there?

J: Umm . . . can I think about it?

M: You're so mean!

J: I'm just kidding. You're fine.

M: So mean!

J: I'm totally kidding. You're the best to tour with. Ever.

M: That's better. Number four: What are some of your favorite memories so far on the tour?

J: I guess performing in Europe for the first time. I had never been to more than two places abroad before, so it was cool seeing England and Germany and Poland and stuff. And I got to perform in an arena in Poland. Oh, but wait—you weren't there for that one.

M: Thanks. So one of your fave memories doesn't include me?

J: Should I come up with another one?

M: Yeah!

J: You asking me twenty questions between shows.

M: Okay, I'll accept that. On to five: Do you ever freak out when we're onstage, like if you forget a lyric or a dance move?

J: Oh yeah. I forget lyrics all the time. I think every time I sing "Never Let You Go" I start to forget the first word and it gives me a little heart attack because it's on the tip of my tongue and I'm blanking.

M: You forgot to catch me yesterday.

J: Oh yeah. Yikes, sorry. But I don't think I was freaking out over that.

M: I was! Question six: Fave city we've been to so far.

J: Probably London. London was really cool because we got to walk around and sightsee, and the energy in the crowd was really good.

M: Number seven: Does it annoy you that I am best friends with your sister Lauren?

J: You guys are always together, but it doesn't really bother me.

M: Not even when we're in the green room before a show making slime?

J: Okay, yeah, that was annoying. That stuff smells, and I think slime in general is gross.

M: Well, we love it—so you're outvoted. Which brings me to eight: Do you feel like Lauren and I gang up on you?

J: You definitely blame things on me. Whenever you make a mess or something, you tell everyone, "It was Johnny!"

M: Number nine: Are you sick of me hanging out at your house all the time?

J: You do come to our house a *lot*. You're always there, but once again, you and Lauren just do stuff all day so I don't really see you. Well, I do see you, obviously, because you're, like, in my living room and you have nowhere else to go. . . .

M: Mean. Again.

J: Truth. Again.

M: We're halfway through this interview.

J: Yesss!

M: Question ten: Do you think boys think and act differently than girls?

J: Uh, yeah. Like completely different. Do I say "like" too much?

M: Now you're asking *me* questions? Get back to mine.

J: I go to school now with regular people, so I'm not constantly around entertainment kids, and I guess I do see some differences between how boys and girls act. There's a lot of chirping among guys, stuff like "I'm better than you." It's kinda weird: Guys *don't* compliment each other and are joking. Girls do compliment each other and are joking.

M: So you're saying guys don't cause as much drama? Or they just don't care as much about what their peers think?

J: Definitely. Both.

M: I think girls hold grudges longer.

J: Yeah, I'm kinda like, "I forgot what we were fighting about, so just drop it."

M: Number eleven: If you could go on a date with one celeb, who would it be?

J: Kylie Jenner.

M: I knew you would say that. So predictable.

J: Kylie's my girl.

M: In your dreams. But she *is* pretty.

J: Understatement.

M: So question twelve: How would you impress a girl? And don't say give her a puppy, because we all know that didn't work out very well.

J: Oh, you mean the Jenzie video? Yeah, I've improved my skills since then.

M: So what would you do?

J: I'm a singer, and girls love when you sing to them. So it's pretty easy for me; I don't even have to hire some guy to sky-write it in the clouds. I just have to start singing, "'Cause if I got you I don't need money.... Girl, you are my heart."

M: And that works for you? Seriously? *Okay...*

J: Don't knock it till ya try it!

M: Number thirteen: Do guys care as much as girls about their clothes?

J: Nah. Unless we're talking shoes.

M: You're all about shoes.

J: Yeah, shoes are sick. And I guess you've got guys who compare themselves—who's the biggest hypebeast. So if you have a Gucci belt, that's really cool.

M: And really weird. What about your hair? That's question fourteen. How long does it take you?

J: Like three minutes. Less.

M: Not true. I've seen you spend at least ten minutes doing your hair.

J: Yeah, but I'm multitasking, so it doesn't count. I'm on the phone or picking music or something.

M: Here's question fifteen: Do you have any idea what concealer or primer is? And no googling the answers.

J: I do! I know what concealer is, because they put it on me when I go on TV. It, like, covers stuff up. What's primer?

M: It goes on before you do your face. It preps you for makeup.

J: And what do they call that stuff that you spray on to set makeup?

M: Setting spray?

J: Makes sense. See, I'm learning lots of very important things during this interview.

M: I once accidentally drank primer. I thought it was something else.

J: That's nasty!

M: It's just water! So . . . number sixteen. We're getting close! Do you like to shop, and if so, for what?

J: Can I say what I hate to shop for?

M: That's changing the question.

J: Okay, I like to shop for shoes, and I hate to shop for furniture. That is the most boring thing in the world.

M: Really? I love that. I love to find stuff to make my home or my room look nice.

J: Are you kidding me?

M: We go to Home Goods, like, every day. What do you like about shoe shopping?

J: That's number seventeen.

M: Fine.

J: I dunno, I get excited shoe shopping. And I like going to Off-White and other hypebeastie stores and looking at all the expensive things.

M: Would you ever splurge? That can be number eighteen.

J: I think I'm going to make a fund, like a whole other bank account for beastie things and save my pennies for them. Then I wouldn't feel so guilty if I wanted to splurge on one. Does that sound reasonable?

M: I guess. Two more questions left!

J: Homestretch!

M: If you were stranded on a deserted island, what's the one thing you couldn't live without?

J: Um, a boat to get me to a non-deserted island?

M: And finally, is there any question you are dying for me to ask you?

J: Do you want anything to eat?

M: That wasn't part of the bargain.

J: Well, you asked....

KENZIE'S CRAFT CORNER

DIY LIP SCRUB

I think this would make a great gift for a boyfriend (kissable lips, lol!) but frankly, I chose it for the guy section of my book because I am always dragging Greg out to Michaels or the grocery store to get the ingredients (so this one's for him!). Because all the ingredients are edible, you can just lick your lips. I love that it's also a breath freshener (and most guys, in my experience, do need a mint!).

WHAT YOU'LL NEED:

* ✳ 2 T sugar
* ✳ 1 tsp. coconut oil
* ✳ ¼ tsp. honey
* ✳ 3-4 drops peppermint
  essential oil

* Mini airtight container
* A small bowl
* A spoon

⎯⎯⎯

1. Place all ingredients in the bowl and mix until combined.
2. Scoop into a small container to store.
3. When you're ready to apply, scoop out about a quarter teaspoon of the scrub and rub on lips in a circular motion. It removes dead, dry skin and leaves lips moisturized and tasty!

ASK KENZIE

Is it really possible to be "just friends" with a boy?

I have plenty of guy friends that I think of like brothers—I would never want to be their girlfriend and they're totally cool with that. If you both agree to keep things in the friend zone, then sure, it can work. But you need to be on the same page; one person can't be crushing. If one of you is (and not being honest about it), it will always get in the way and make things awkward and uncomfortable.

I'm fourteen and a freshman in high school, but my parents think I'm too young to have a boyfriend! Help!

It's weird in my family: My mom is actually okay with me having a boyfriend *in concept*, but my stepdad, Greg, would freak. We can't tell him. But then there are times when they are both overprotective of me because I'm the youngest and they still want me to be a baby. If I like a boy, my mom will send Maddie with me to check him out! My mom is like, "Maddie, watch her every move." Does she think I'm gonna run off somewhere and elope? I think it's just hard for parents to wrap their heads around the fact that we're growing up. If you have a boyfriend, that's one step closer to marriage—and they can't deal with losing you. I'd say take it one step at a time. If you do like a boy, then introduce him to your family so they get to know him and see how nice he is.

How can I impress this boy I think is cute?

Be yourself—that's the best way to win him over. If you try and act like someone you're not just to impress him, it might work at first, but I promise you, eventually he'll figure out you're faking. I know this girl who absolutely *hated* football but told her BF she loved it—just so he'd ask her out. Well, it worked. But guess where she wound up every Sunday to make him happy? Sitting on his couch watching football games! She was bored and eventually realized they had absolutely

nothing in common. That was the end of that relationship! The moral of this story is, don't shy away from
showing your personality because you're scared some
boy will reject you. If he doesn't like the real you, then
he's not worthy.

RULE 10
WRITE YOUR OWN RULES

"NOW IT'S YOUR TURN!"

Which means I give you permission to take all the things I've taught you in this book and make them your own. Twist them, bend them, put your own personal spin on them. Don't let people discourage you from "doing you." My mom always says, "There's only one Kenzie," and there have been times I needed to "Kenzie-fy" a situation, i.e., do a little rule-rewriting. Case in point: One time I was competing at a dance competition and I totally forgot my dance—blanked. I knew I wasn't supposed to change the choreo (that is a serious rule my dance coaches always enforced), but I couldn't just sit there onstage, staring at the judges! So I made something up; I did a chin stand and I wound up facing a totally different direction than I was supposed to be in. You know what? It worked! So I bent the rules a little. I put my own spin on a dance routine and it was okay. I was proud of myself for improvising. I know that if I break any rules in the future, it will be for a very good reason (e.g., a potential disaster) and I'll do it in a way that's authentically me. Rules are made to keep kids safe—I get that. But as we grow up, and we're able to judge and make smart, educated decisions for ourselves, there's a little wiggle room in there, don't ya think? Hey, Mom, are you reading this, lol?

The only rule that you should *never* break is to be true to yourself. In fact, that's the best reason for you to challenge the rules that already exist in the world—if they go against who you are and what you think and believe. There's no one else like you, and your life, your dreams, your career, they're all yours to decide. So let me see what you've got! I also want to leave you with one last thing to think about.

KENZIE'S 6 SIMPLE RULES FOR BEING HAPPY

1. Love, don't hate.

2. Work hard and you'll be great.

3. Give, don't just take.

4. Have fun—and make mistakes!

5. Be a kind and caring friend.

6. Follow your dreams till the very end!

So I think that says it all—and it rhymes, lol! I hope you remember my rules as you go through every day of your journey. I know I'm always excited to see what tomorrow will hold and how I will tackle it. It's like, "Okay, universe! Take your best shot! I'm ready for you!" I'm sure there'll be lots more tough stuff that comes up—I'm only thirteen, after all. But that's okay—I'll make new rules to live by to get me through it. The world we live in is changing so fast, just like we are. It helps me a lot just thinking how, as teens, we all go through so many of the same challenges. Our parents did too, and guess what? They survived! Our generation is even stronger, smarter, and more powerful than the ones that have come before us, so we're going to be just fine. In fact, we're gonna be awesome!

ACKNOWLEDGMENTS

Wow. I can't believe it ... I've finished this whole book! I had so much fun doing it, but I definitely couldn't have done it without help.

Sharon, Mel, Joe, Jenni, Erin, and everyone at WME, thanks for helping me find my own voice and my own path. You guys have been amazing and I really can't thank you enough!

Natasha, you are an amazing editor! Thank you for helping me say what I wanted to say in the best way. And thanks to Jen B., Jen L., Jen R., Hannah, and everyone at Gallery Books and Simon & Schuster. Without you guys I know this book couldn't have happened and I really appreciate everything you have done for me and this project!

Sheryl, sometimes I think you know me better than I know myself! I loved talking to you and writing with you. Now I just need you to get a duet with me ;)

There are so many friends to say thank you to . . . In Pittsburgh, LA, Canada, all over . . . You guys are the best, and thanks for always supporting me, making me have fun, and listening to me. I love you!!

To the ALDC, Lifetime, and Collins Avenue, thank you for letting a little firecracker like me be a part of a wild ride.

Rachel, you do so much for me and my whole family. I honestly don't know what we would do without you. Thank you for everything. Always.

Michelle, I will never be able to thank you enough for helping me grow as a musician and fall even more in love with music.

Kelly-Marie, thanks for always standing by me and making sure even the longest night is a lot of fun.

Scott, Sarah, Miles, and my entire amazing legal team—thank you so much for all that you do.

Jane, Jack, and Lilia, thanks for letting me always be at your house—even when you're not home . . . AND for the endless Limonata and trampolining . . . I love you guys!

Mommy Meredith, you're like my second mom and I love spending so much time with you, Lauren, Johnny, and Dale. Love you!!

Maddie, I know we may fight sometimes but you are honestly my best friend in the whole world. I don't know what I would do without you. I love you more than I could say and you are the best big sister ever.

Gregga, you will stop at nothing to make me happy. From Target runs to ice cream runs to being patient during school, sometimes I don't know how you do it! I love you even more than Maliboo loves you!

Mom, you are just the best. You do so much for me and Maddie. All day, every day. You always put us first and I know I would be lost without you. Thank you for everything, always. I love you so so much!!